Table of Contents

Foreword

I was Doris Day's personal secretary in Hollywood from 1971-1974. For many months during the period 1972-1974 I lived in her home, becoming the only person outside her family to do so for any period of time.

The 70s were key years for this famous and world-acclaimed actress. It was a decade in which, having just completed a stellar career in the movies, she filmed a TV series, experienced widowhood and fought for her financial future, re-connected with her son, and began the animal-rights efforts that would distinguish her for the rest of her life.

Before I was her secretary and, I believe, her friend, I was a young girl from a Catholic family in the Midwest, just as Doris had been. She had her favorite movie stars; I did too: Ginger Rogers was her idol, Doris Day, mine. I learned to be interested in people and celebrities as a newspaper reporter in Indianapolis. Most of all I was Doris Day's fan. This is the story of my experiences through a journey to fanhood and into a world of famous people and interesting experiences I could never have predicted. It is told in personal detail and from my own memories.

After Lauren Benjamin, one of our original Day Gang and a neighbor, encouraged me to be interviewed by David Kaufman, a New York author doing a book on Doris due out in mid-2008, I thought of my Day years anew. Maybe it was the reporter in me, but I had kept great notes. I realized that Doris is now an historical figure, and my story a slice of history. Certainly during those years I tried to be a good secretary by keeping my daily journals up to date, along with documents and records from my work with her. These are the basis of my story.

For a long time I was out of fan mode. I have been in contact with Doris briefly over the years by letter, but not recently. She was kind enough to send a note to me after my mother died, which I cherish. Most of all, though, it is the memories of those years with this remarkable woman and human being that I cherish the most.

Day at a Time

An Indiana Girl's Sentimental Journey to
Doris Day's Hollywood and Beyond

To Mary,
Enjoy!
Maryanne Barothy

Mary Anne Barothy

Hawthorne Publishing
Carmel, Indiana

ISBN: 978-0-9787167-3-8 Hardcover
ISBN: 978-0-9787167-4-5 Softcover

For information contact:
Hawthorne Publishing
15601 Oak Road
Carmel, Indiana 46033
(317) 867-5183
www.hawthornepub.com

Printed and bound in the United States of America

Acknowledgments

My journey to completing this book has depended upon many people. I wrote the first draft over 32 years ago while in California and brought it back to Indianapolis where it sat in a box in my garage. Lauren Benjamin encouraged me to tell the story fully, and my largest "thank you" must go to her.

None of this story would ever have happened if it were not for Eileen Freshwater-Koford, who invited me to California and encouraged me with stories of her visits with our idol. Thanks also to Mary, my friend and former roommate, who along with Hilda and Eileen, welcomed me into their Day Gang. We had great times, now great memories.

I want to express appreciation also to the following people for their interest and advice: Jackie Joseph; Rona Barrett; Joan Bey, whom I have known from Indiana Press Women for many years; Lawrence S. "Bo" Connor, author and former Managing Editor for *The Indianapolis Star*; Bonnie Britton, movie critic for *The Star*; and Nelson Price, the popular Indiana author who led me to Nancy and Art Baxter of Hawthorne Publishing. I owe a great debt of gratitude to Nancy, a veteran of over 20 years of book publishing, who has worked closely with me these past months to bring this sentimental journey to fruition.

Thanks also goes to Claude Anderson for taking time to review this work and Elizabeth Chepules, who helped improve it.

Special appreciation goes to J. Denis Glover, former Lifestyle Editor of *The Christian Science Monitor,* who served as vital member of this team at all the latter stages. His sound advice and keen eye were real assets.

Last, and of course most importantly, I must thank Doris Day for allowing me to live for a while a life beyond my dearest dream.

1

A Fifties Fan

Why Doris Day? That blond, sharp-shooting, rambunctious lady in *Calamity Jane* attracted my attention—belting out songs and executing high jinks— jumping on horses, tables, and wagons—always smiling a gorgeous smile. That was my earliest recollection of Doris Day in her legendary performance in the Warner Brothers hit about the mythic American west. At age 10 in 1954, I watched it with my mother and a friend, and the singing and dancing so appealed to me that I saw the movie several more times.

Maybe it was her beautiful singing voice, maybe the roles she played. However, three years later in 1957, I noticed a display of 45 rpm records on the magazine rack at the local Kroger's. Doris Day's "Columbia Hall of Fame" series record sat right on top, staring at me. Her smiling face made me beg my mother to buy the record. I had to have Doris Day sing for me in my own home.

I played "Pretty Baby" over and over. I'm still not sure if it was the lilting way she sang or her inviting face on the cover that hooked me, but I was a Doris Day fan at 10.

Perhaps the association had formed earlier. When I was only six months old living in St. Paul, Ruth Green, our teen-aged next-door neighbor, played Doris Day's "Sentimental Journey" repeatedly. Ruth's bedroom window faced my nursery. Since no one had air conditioning and the summer windows stood open, you heard everything. I once told Doris about this introduction to her and her music before I was one year old. She commented

"Marzy, [her nickname for me], do you realize that I was singing and working years before you were born?"

Elvis, Pat Boone, Ricky Nelson, and Annette became all the rage in 1958 when I was an eighth grader at Christ the King Grade School in Indianapolis. Pat and Ricky were two of my favorites, and I bought all their records, too. Doris Day photos cut from movie magazines covered my bulletin board and bedroom walls, and I had a mini-movie-star museum with pictures from their latest movies. My friends, Jeanne Conrad and Carole Ahr, and I bought *Photoplay*, which told about Doris's newest movies and went into details of her family life, sometimes describing her son Terry. We shared the magazines breathlessly, reading each from cover to cover, wondering what it would be like to know the stars.

Born in Illinois, I grew up in a middle-class Catholic home in Indianapolis. My parents saw to it that my brother John and I were educated in parochial schools, and we attended church every Sunday and on special holy days. Many of our friends shared common interests, and two of those were the movies and TV. Our house was one of the first on our block to have a television set, and sometimes neighbor kids came to watch.

The Golden Age of the movies was coming to a close in the mid 50s, with TV starting to make a big impact. In the early 1950s the black and white screen mesmerized me, and "I Love Lucy" on CBS became my big favorite. Every Monday night John and I were glued to the set in our living room for her weekly show. I addressed the first fan letter I ever wrote to Lucy Ricardo. I discovered what I took to be her home address, only to find out when the letter returned weeks later, there was "no such person." I was too young to realize "Ricardo" was only Lucille Ball's TV-show name.

After my parents took us to see the 1954 movie *The Long, Long Trailer*, starring Lucy and Desi, my brother and I were so fascinated that we begged Mom and Dad to get a trailer. To pacify us, they took us to look at some motor homes on West Washington Street, the business address of several trailer dealerships. But they had no intention of purchasing one—to our disappointment. Doris's *Calamity Jane* came out that year, and those two movies made an indelible impression on me.

As we entered our teens, my poor parents had to endure constant music blaring from our bedrooms. My brother John's music, especially "Wipe Out!" by the Surfaris and "Let There Be Drums" by Sandy Nelson, boomed out from his room. But the Friday night, Saturday night, and matinee movies stood at the top of my entertainment list. And Doris Day shone at the pinnacle of my star chart.

My fascination with Doris grew as I got older. *Photoplay* ran a story on fan clubs, and I immediately sent away for information on how to find a Doris Day club. A faded Xerox reply soon arrived with the address of the Doris Day Society in London. Oddly enough, no club existed in the US.

I promptly wrote a letter to the secretary, Sheila Smith, and she sent me a membership form, the current quarterly *Journal*, and a small black-and-white photo of Doris. I was happy to be in the club and, better yet, to hear from other members all over the world about their experiences with Doris. Some had actually met her and wrote articles for the *Journal*. I eagerly awaited each issue and read and re-read every single story until the magazine became tattered.

Eventually, I wrote a couple of articles for the London club's newsletter and sent them off to Sheila, including an open letter to Doris, which I spent a lot of time on because I really wanted her to read it. Thrilled to see it in the next issue, I believed Doris would see it, too, because, according to Sheila, she did read each issue. I was determined she would know my name. Mary Anne Barothy. Remember that, Doris!

I attended St. Agnes Academy, an all-girls high school run by the Sisters of Providence near downtown in Indianapolis. There I added to my collection of Doris Day records and photos. As the high school years unfolded, I became ever more of an avid fan, writing numerous letters to Doris, hoping for a personal reply. At first I had only a studio address, but when I actually found her home address printed in a movie magazine, I became ecstatic and mailed my letters directly to her. All I received in return, however, was the studio photo post cards with printed signatures, postmarked from either Beverly Hills or Cincinnati. Later I found out that Doris's mom, Alma Day, and Doris's Aunt Marie (her mother's sister in Cincinnati) sent many of these replies while on vacation in Cincinnati, the Days' home ground. Alma told me they used to take bags of fan mail with them on the train and sit for hours sending out these cards.

Born Doris Mary Ann Von Kapplehoff in Cincinnati, Doris confided years later that when she was a young girl, her favorite movie star was Ginger Rogers. She adored the tap-dancing beauty, and as a fan she sent many letters to Ginger, often including money. She never received a reply. I guess that was why she was eager that her fans at least received a photo, even if only a postcard.

When about 14 or 15 and eager for any connection to Doris, I found the address of one of her relatives in Cincinnati, Jeanne Welz, and wrote to her. To my surprise, she answered with a cordial letter and a color photo of Doris and her husband, Marty Melcher, taken in the living room of relatives in Cincinnati in 1957 during the premiere of her hit film *Julie*, also starring Louis Jordan. Faded now, the photo is in my special album on Doris.

Since my interest in Doris began in the late 50s and I had missed her early movies on the big screen, I yearned to see them. The Emerson Theater, about ten miles from my home, ran a lot of old films, including many starring Doris. I tried everything I knew to get to the Emerson, constantly begging my parents to drive me. Sometimes they gave in and drove across town; other times they didn't. Mournfully I ended up at home playing Doris's records, but it was not the same.

The first week I ventured to the Emerson, it was showing the MGM musical *Love Me Or Leave Me* from 1955, starring Doris and James Cagney. I was eager to see it on the big screen. After a while I became a "regular" at the theater and made friends with the manager, a Mr. Johnson, a kind, understanding man who would often give me the Doris movie posters and stills when the movie run closed. One Saturday afternoon my mother accompanied me to see *Love Me Or Leave Me* again. I chatted with Johnson at the box office. During the middle of the movie, we saw someone coming toward us with a flashlight. My mother panicked—we couldn't tell who it was or what was happening. It was Mr. Johnson with one of the big marquee movie posters rolled under his arm. He wanted to make sure I had it before we left.

Being an alert fan and having the help of the fan club with all the "inside scoop" on Doris's movies, I knew when her movies and records were to be released. I was constantly on the phone with movie distributors to find out the exact date for the opening of a show. I marked my calendar as the countdown began, preparing to be there when the doors opened.

I became friends with a man who worked at the one record shop, Ballinger Records, near my home and always the first to get Doris Day releases. Invariably, I was his first sale each time a new release appeared. Whenever we went on vacation, I checked out record stores, Salvation Army outlets, and junk shops for my favorite singer's records. Sometimes I got lucky and purchased a collector's item for a nickel. All of her 78 rpm records dropped out of print with Columbia, and I was constantly on the lookout for them.

In my quest to enlarge my collection, I tracked down a sympathetic man in the publicity department at Columbia Records in New York. He periodically sent me record covers from Doris's new LP's, and about twice a year I received a large tube with several inside. I was thrilled with the new addition to my bulging collection and placed one of each on my bedroom walls, much to the chagrin of my parents.

Inscriptions in my St. Agnes Academy High School freshman yearbook say, "To Jane Osgood, Doris Day's Number One Fan." "Osgood" was the name of the character Doris played in the 1959 picture *It Happened to Jane,* co-starring Jack Lemmon. These inscriptions demonstrated how far my fanmania had progressed. I was known as "Doris Day the Second" or "Jane Osgood" by some of the girls and also by a local DJ. I must have seen the Jane movie in which Doris plays a New England lobster woman at least 10 times and had memorized almost the whole script.

A favorite teacher, Sister Thomas Aquinas, (TA to us) who taught Latin, let it be known that she thought I should spend my time studying instead of concentrating all my time on Doris Day. My parents agreed. No one, no adult, that is, could understand my devotion to this blond person in far-off Hollywood. I can hear my parents saying, "If only you would spend as much time on your homework as you do on Doris Day, you could be a great student." Their carping did not diminish my love of my heroine. One of my dad's favorite satiric comments was, "I'll call the Pope to have Doris Day canonized." Eventually, they began to realize that their daughter was a stubborn fanatic with a one-track mind, so they let me alone with it.

In the late 50s the Legion of Decency, a Catholic organization that rated movies for families, gave Doris's 1957 *Pajama Game* movie a "B" rating, similar to an "R" rating today. When TA learned that I had seen it, she asked, "Why did you go to see that dirty movie?" I replied, "I read the book, I saw the play, and I like Doris Day." This did not sit well.

Later the same year, I got into more trouble. Taking photos of nuns was not allowed. A friend of mine, Kathy, knew I had taken a photo of TA and traded that photo for a shoe box of Doris Day photos. I enjoyed my newly acquired box of Day items. Things went well until TA learned she had been traded for Doris. That did it! I was put on probation for a couple of weeks. In the 1980s I renewed my friendship with TA, who was now called "Sister

Beth." We laughed about that incident that happened many years ago, and I let her know she remains one of my favorite people, surely the equal of Doris. Sister Beth at age 91 continues to be an inspiration to me today.

One day a photo of Doris appeared in a Wasson's department store ad. Their beauty salon offered a hairdo designed to make the customer look like Doris Day. I phoned immediately for an appointment, but though I emerged with my hair poufed and turned under, I never came close to looking like Doris.

I was graduated from St. Agnes in 1962 and that summer began working for a local department store where many friends were already employed. I clerked in women's ready-to-wear and began putting money aside for college. Still, I cherished a dream of a trip to California. I had formulated a plan to meet the stars I so idolized.

It wasn't all about Doris. Any bright face that popped up on the big and little screen became fair game. I also admired Carol Burnett, a rising star on the popular "Garry Moore Show." During the summer of 1962, I read that Carol was coming for a week to Starlight Musicals, an outdoor summer theater featuring variety shows with top performers. Carol would be doing a solo show similar to the one she had done with Julie Andrews at Carnegie Hall earlier in the year. I called my friend Jan Moore at the *Indianapolis Times*, who also sent me Carol Burnett photos, and asked if I could possibly take a photo of Carol for her. I told her I had front row seats, and after checking me out, she invited me to go with her to meet Carol at the airport.

August 6, 1962, my mother dropped me off at the *Times* building, and Jan and I rode in a black Rolls Royce to meet Carol's flight from Detroit. Jan introduced me to her, and Carol proved most gracious in posing for photos. To my surprise the evening edition of the *Indianapolis Times* carried Jan's lead story, "Hoosier Hello Stuns Carol Burnett," along with a photo of Carol and me. I had taken my snapshots and visited with Carol. Sadly, at the bottom of the page appeared a photo and story about Marilyn Monroe's shocking death.

The following year on September 22, 1963, my brother John's photo plastered the front page of the same newspaper with the tragic story of the fatal car accident that took him and his girlfriend the night before. We were all devastated by his untimely death at age 17. He was graduated from Cathedral High School across from St. Agnes June, 1963, and left for

Indiana State University in Terre Haute, two weeks before. That was his first weekend home from college. My parents took his death very hard and unconsciously may have clung to me more than ever. It was a rough time for all of us.

In 1964 when my parents and I spent a week at the New York World's Fair, I contacted Carol Burnett about seeing her after her Broadway show, *Fade Out–Fade In,* co-starring Jack Cassidy, at the Mark Hellinger Theater, and she agreed to see me. On July 15, 1964, with the matinee over, we left the theater and headed for the stage door through a mob of people eagerly waiting with autograph books. While I made my way through, my parents stood under a tree in the shade, thinking I would never make any contact. As soon as I got to the door, the guard announced, "The only person allowed backstage is Mary Anne Barothy." After I entered, she insisted I bring my parents in, too.

In nearly two hours of visiting, I showed Carol the photos I brought from her visit to Indianapolis. "You have more photos of me than my grandmother," she joked. It was a vivid, personal encounter with one of my favorite luminaries. My father had not been that interested in all of this "fan-stuff," but by the time the afternoon ended, he was a big Carol Burnett fan, too.

But my dream continued to be meeting Doris. Through the Doris Day Society, I started writing to many pen pals, exchanging ideas with some of the people who had actually met her. One girl, Eileen from Canton, Ohio, had many stories printed in the *Journal* about her California trip. We corresponded and then met. She shared wonderful stories of Doris and Marty at the LA Dodgers and LA Lakers games. This was the closest I had ever been to anyone who met Doris, and I hung onto every word. I envied Eileen as she drove off the next morning. I wanted to be a stowaway. In my heart I knew that one day I'd be heading west, too.

Doris climbed to the pinnacle of her movie career during this period. She had a string of hit movies, *Pillow Talk* with Rock Hudson in 1959, *Please Don't Eat the Daisies* with David Niven in 1960, *Midnight Lace* with Rex Harrison in 1960, *Lover Come Back* with Rock Hudson in 1961, *That Touch of Mink* with Cary Grant 1962, and *The Thrill of It All* and *Move Over Darling* with James Garner, both in 1963. Doris had married her third husband, Marty Melcher, her manager, on her birthday in 1951. Until now, little had been written about her teen-aged son Terry at Principia, a boarding school in Missouri. Doris's singing career still went strong, and between films she recorded successful albums.

All this time my parents hoped I would outgrow the movie-star stage. They said I needed to become interested in more cultural things. Still, for my part I was not a one-note band at all, going to college where I did well. I worked part time and dated occasionally. But in the back of my mind burned the desire to become friends with the lady I admired so much. The ground work had been laid, and I prepared for "something" in my future.

My mother Rose and I sat for a portrait in St. Paul, Minnesota.

Sister Junie, parents Charles and Rose Barothy, and I pose circa 1945.

The two Barothy children admire the family nativity scene about 1948.

I am dressed up for my sister's wedding on July 16, 1949.

My brother John and I in 1951. Note my doll that looked like early Doris Day.

My graduation from St. Agnes Academy, June, 1962, left me with a diploma and a desire to go west.

The front page of the Indianapolis Times *shows me presenting a scrapbook to Carol Burnett on August 6, 1962.*

I was able to be with Carol Burnett after the Broadway show, Fade Out-Fade In, *in the summer of 1964.*

2

California, Here I Come!

The next three years I kept up with Doris via calls and letters from Eileen, my friend from the Doris Day Society, who finally settled in West Los Angeles. I was at Marian College in Indianapolis, pursuing English and Journalism, but I wanted to graduate from college and move to California, and nothing was going to stop me, not even a love interest. In my junior year I began dating another student, Les. We got pretty serious, but I didn't want to stay in the Midwest at that time, and he, unfortunately, couldn't understand. I had my sights set on going west, so we deferred our romance.

Finally, after much planning, the day arrived to fly to Los Angeles, August 15, 1965, at the height of the Watts Riots.

The ominous headline in *The Indianapolis Star* screamed, "Planes Being Shot Down at LA Airport." My parents were a wreck knowing I headed for Los Angeles on that sunny Sunday afternoon, and they begged me not to. But despite the confusion and conflict, I was determined to pursue my dream.

Eileen invited me to come to LA and stay with her and her roommate Hilda at their Bundy Drive apartment in West Los Angeles. Mary joined them from Long Beach, and another avid fan, Lauren from Denver, came to welcome me. It was a mini-Doris Day convention!

We cruised by Doris's home in Beverly Hills at 713 Crescent Drive more than once. In fact, we must have ended up driving by a dozen times that day, hoping to catch a glimpse of the movie queen or just see any activity at all. In a sneaky "Lucy and Ethel" scenario, we even drove down her alley to see what she threw out. Our biggest fear was that someone would stop us or think we were trespassing, but we managed to finish our tour without complications.

Lauren and I fell speechless when Eileen and Hilda shared photos from Catalina Island, where they saw Doris filming *The Glass Bottom Boat,* co-starring Rod Taylor and Arthur Godfrey, for MGM. Doris sat on her bike, and Eileen and Hilda stood on either side of her. Mary had photos of herself with Doris taken at a Dodger game and talked about running into her in the ladies' room. All agreed that Doris treated them graciously each time they met her, taking time to chat.

Mary's father often drove her from Long Beach to Beverly Hills to spend time walking by Doris's in the hope of catching a glimpse of Miss Day. Mary recalled one time while standing near Doris's home, the star came out and quizzed her asking, "Mary, what are you doing here?" To which she answered, "I was just in the neighborhood." Doris looked in amazement and exclaimed, "But you live in Long Beach!"

In those innocent decades movie stars more fully interacted with their public. Occasionally we saw the American dancer Fred Astaire driving his Rolls Royce, or popular actresses of the 40s and 50s, Rosalind Russell, at the Food Giant grocery store, and screen legend Loretta Young at Good Shepherd Catholic Church in Beverly Hills, or the king of the one-liners, stand-up comedian, Henny Youngman at Nate 'N Al's restaurant. Doris, an avid cyclist and health enthusiast, often rode her red, ten-speed bike freely through the streets of Beverly Hills unnoticed, with no paparazzi hounding her every move.

Prior to my trip west, I had written many letters to Doris's secretary Phyllis, asking to meet Doris during my two-week vacation. I knew she was filming *Glass Bottom Boat* at MGM, and I asked about a studio tour. Phyllis wrote that she would try to set up a meeting, but could not promise anything. She did arrange an MGM studio tour for us, where we saw the *Harlow* set and many other behind-the-scene sound stages. But I still had not met my favorite star. The day we toured the studio, Doris was filming on Catalina Island. The day we took the steamer to Catalina, Doris came back to the MGM lot.

I often had to pinch myself. Beverly Hills was definitely not the

Midwest! I fell in love with the tall, graceful palm trees lining many streets; the meticulously landscaped mansions were all so different and colorful. Despite clouds or smog in the early morning, we could always look forward to plenty of sun by mid-morning. And people seemed so much more relaxed, both in dress and attitude, that it was easy to fall into this lifestyle. In no time I felt at home.

Lauren, Mary, and I passed Doris's home in Beverly Hills numerous times each day and "tooled" around to Malibu to see her beach home on Pacific Coast Highway. On one of the Malibu trips I learned the silent screen movie star Doris was named after, Doris Kenyon, lived two blocks south of her on Crescent Drive. Even though I never saw Doris Day on my first trip, I found wonderful friends who shared my love for her, and we bonded immediately. My past life in Indianapolis—going to school, dating, and working—seemed dull compared to the glamour of California. Still I needed to go back and resume life beyond the bright lights. I returned to Indianapolis with renewed hope for another trip the following year. I was certainly "California Dreamin'."

Through a relative Mary had access to free long-distance calls, so we spent hours on the phone. I looked forward to each call from Mary, knowing I would get more first-hand news on comings, goings, and showings. Any time she saw Doris, Mary would call and fill me in. Doris, after releasing a series of very popular films and receiving large amounts of money for a star, had put her previous marriages, the first to Al Jordan and the second to George Weidler, behind her. She was living under the almost constant "management" of her strong-minded husband Marty, who continued to press her to take on movie after movie. Her final movie in 1968 was her 39th in twenty years!

Unofficially we formed our own "Day Gang." From afar some of us remembered Doris with a gift on special occasions, pooling our money so the girls in Los Angeles could make purchases. One time Doris invited the local gang to the studio, and they presented her with a beautiful silver tea service. I have a studio photo with Doris in the middle holding our tea service and the girls on either side. She sent me a thank-you note, as I belonged to that group, too. I marveled when I saw that photo back in my Indiana home. The girls were on the set with Doris! They called me shortly after, bubbly with enthusiasm, and told me about their "glorious Day with Doris."

During my senior year at Marian—taking classes in journalism, fashion illustration, and French, still dating Les—that cool, sun-drenched lifestyle kept calling me. Les and I attended the senior prom and the Indianapolis 500 that year, the year of the horrible crash just before the start of the race. We had excellent seats in the first turn, and I saw the pile-up through the lens of my 8mm movie camera.

Several of my college friends were girls I'd also known from St. Agnes. We all had big dreams. Theirs included a husband, a ranch home, about five kids, and possibly a teaching job. I had my mind set on living where people strolled beaches and ate tacos. I graduated from Marian in June of 1966. Les proposed to me, but I had to refuse. "I'm sorry Les. I'm moving to California one day soon." That was the end of our romance.

I visited LA again the summer of 1966, when Doris was filming *Caprice* at Twentieth Century Fox. The Day Gang toured the various stops, hoping to catch a glimpse of her, but to no avail. Since the girls had seen Doris many times, I listened intently as each told her story. During this trip I caught up on all the news and returned home with the hope that the next time I ventured to LA would be "the" time for me to meet the lady I had admired for some twelve years.

3

Third Time is the Charm

Late in 1966 a friend at L. S. Ayres department store told me about a position at *The Indianapolis News*, now the city's only afternoon newspaper. *The News* was the Great Hoosier Daily, for more than 60 years honored in Indianapolis for strong coverage of the community and human-interest stories. I interviewed and became a reporter for the women's society page.

I handled the brides and wedding announcements, did feature stories when needed, and covered the Saturday night "Bourbon beat." I'll never forget the thrill of seeing my first by-line on October 21, 1967, when I covered the Harkness Ballet Premiere at Clowes Hall at Butler University. I still have a copy of that story. I loved the variety and excitement of working at *The News*. Finally, I had an authentic press pass, which gave me entree to otherwise forbidden territory.

One memorable interview came in 1967 with Sonny and Cher in their dressing room at what is now Pepsi Coliseum on the Indiana State Fairgrounds. They dressed in shimmering pink satin outfits, which Cher said she had created. While we leisurely talked before their show, I heard a knock at the door. Cher opened it to Glen Campbell, an up-and-coming recording star, who asked if he could be on the show with them. Glen had just driven from an Ohio gig, after learning they were doing a show in Indianapolis. They welcomed him and put on a great performance to the delight of the packed Coliseum. "I Got You, Babe" brought down the house.

I was learning to be at ease with celebrities. They were human, too.

During October, I flew to the west coast again. My friends in Los Angeles had spoken to Doris about my trip, and to my surprise, she said she would like to meet me!

The day before I left, my newspaper friends cautioned, "Doris is a very hard person to see." Charlie Staff, the entertainment editor, knew that for a fact. I understood they said all this for my own good, but this time was going to be different.

When I landed late in the afternoon, Mary came to meet me. We drove to Eileen's and Hilda's West LA apartment, where I met three charming Australian girls from the Doris Day Society Down Under. Mary told me she had seen Doris earlier in the week and mentioned I was coming to town and would really love to meet her. Doris had seemed most agreeable and talked about getting together at Bailey's Bakery, a little shop she frequented when not working. Doris never gave Mary a definite day, so we decided not to take any chances and headed for Bailey's every morning, waiting for her famous red bike.

The Bailey's routine became part of Doris Day mythology. When she was not working, as on Saturdays, or when on hiatus from making movies, she loved to hop on her bike and ride to the bakery. She enjoyed visiting with Hilda Turner, the congenial, middle-aged manager, and chatting with the regulars who stopped in for hot coffee or tea and one of the bakery's delicious, homemade decadent pastries: eclairs, Bavarian cakes, or bear claws. Doris got exercise riding her bike, especially uphill to her home. Streets in that era were not as congested as today's, and she rode with ease, often on the sidewalk, especially on Canon and Beverly Drive. Rarely did anyone stop her.

So Mary and I got up early Thursday and drove to Bailey's in hopes Doris would arrive. Sipping coffee and nibbling sweet rolls, we waited impatiently. Every time the door opened, we expected to see Doris bouncing in. As the noon hour approached, we decided something must have come up, but Mary insisted Doris really had expressed an interest in meeting me.

Only one more day, Saturday, remained in the week, but we had not wasted our time coming in this way. We chatted with several regular customers who saw Doris frequently, especially when not filming. I didn't want to seem too much like a fan; still, I took in every word about her from those who knew her. Most who frequented Bailey's were older business people who came to the village for a coffee break or people just stopping in for take-out pastries in that wonderful atmosphere smelling of cinnamon and bread baking. Those stopping for take-outs left with neatly tied white boxes.

Saturday morning arrived, and we rose early. Sharing one bathroom to do our hair and shower, we had to be up with the chickens and work in shifts in order to be ready to go by 9:00 AM. We knew Doris was also an early bird, wishing to get to the bakery as soon as possible. We chose a large booth in the corner, perfect for all of us. Once the girls sat, room remained for two more—Doris and me. We must have looked like a production company, with cameras of all shapes and sizes.

I purposely sat with my back to the door, but the others could see anyone who came in, so they teased me. Each time it creaked open, one would say, "Oh, Mary Anne, here's Doris!" Hearing this several times only to find an old lady or someone else, I didn't pay any attention. But after a long pause, the girls beamed and called, "Mary Anne, here she is." Believing they were up to their old tricks, I paid no attention and bit into my sweet roll.

Suddenly I heard that famous husky voice, "Well, hello, Mary Anne! How are you?" She went on to say she knew the girls, so I had to be Mary Anne. I choked on my roll but slowly turned around, trying to compose myself. She didn't have the bouffant hairdo I was used to seeing in the movies nor was she dressed up. And what happened to all those freckles? Dressed in beige walking shorts, a pink-and-white checked cap, pink turtleneck sweater, and a beautiful leather jacket, she looked quite comfortable, as natural and down-to-earth as I had hoped; and she seemed quite at home with all of us.

I don't know if it was the reporter in me or the curious fan, but I immediately began asking questions: "When will you make another album? What's your next movie?" She answered everything with enthusiasm. The girls moved down to another table and let Doris and me have a chance to get to know one another. It was thoughtful, since everyone knew I was scheduled to fly home the next day. Doris asked what I did, and I told her I reported for *The Indianapolis News*. I also mentioned that my parents were not happy with the prospect of my moving to Los Angeles. Doris encouraged me, "Tell your parents you want to move. You're 23 and certainly old enough to start making your own plans."

While we chatted, the girls began taking photos. I was eager to show the results to my colleagues at *The News*, all those nay-sayers who had told me Doris would be hard to reach.

I think the nicest part of the whole meeting was that Doris made us feel so much at ease, like long-lost friends. She was not a snob, but very warm, and sincerely seemed to enjoy herself with us. My fan dreams from all those years had begun to be realized.

Doris mentioned that as soon as Marty came back from their office, she would have to leave. They would ride bikes home. I dreaded to see that bike appear, but eventually I heard her say, "Oh, there's Marty. I'll have to be going, but I want you girls to meet him." We walked out together, and she began introducing him to all of us. When my turn came, she said, "Marty, this is Mary Anne from Indianapolis. She's a reporter."

I don't know what ran through his mind, but as soon as he heard the word "reporter" his pleasant expression changed. He had always arranged her interviews and surely thought I was doing a "without permission" story. Marty looked at me and then at Doris, and she could sense his displeasure. She quickly added, "Marty, Mary Anne's my friend." He then realized this was just another "fan club" meeting. I asked if I could take a photo of them. She went to him and posed by his bike; they looked happy together. Doris hugged each of us goodbye.

Marty stood about six feet with dark hair and a strong physique. He had been her manager since 1951. He seemed very businesslike, and he revealed that when he assumed I was a reporter trying to get a scoop. Still, he was pleasant enough. I felt hopeful that in the future I might be able to contact him about working for their production company, Arwin Productions, which handled Doris's movies and music.

As the Melchers rode off on the sidewalk, we stood outside Bailey's watching. Now that the party was over, I realized I was running late for a luncheon date with Durward Kirby, co-star of the popular TV variety "Garry Moore Show," and his lovely wife Pax at their home in the Hollywood Hills, friends from my Indianapolis experience.

The Kirbys : Durward and Pax

I had met Durward and Pax Kirby seven years earlier in 1960 in Indianapolis while he was second banana for Garry Moore. While still in high school, I was asked to write letters for an elderly lady, Mrs. Frank Young, who had a severe case of arthritis and could not write her own personal letters. Every Sunday after attending Mass at Christ the King Catholic Church, I went around the corner to the Youngs' residence. On my first visit I learned that Youngs' daughter, Mary Paxton, had married Durward. Whenever the Kirbys visited, Mrs. Young invited me. Pax and Durward, very congenial people, came to look on me as a daughter. Their older son Randy was two years older than I, and Dennis, their younger son, five years my junior. They had recently moved to California to live. When Mrs. Young mentioned I was going to Los Angeles for a visit, Pax invited me to lunch the same Saturday I met Doris. A weekend of celebrities.

I'm with Durward Kirby at the Kirby home in Sanibel, Florida, about 1984. We were friends for many years.

I returned to Indianapolis, but not for long. After my conversations with Doris, I knew I was going to move to Los Angeles as soon as I could make arrangements. I dreaded telling my parents, depriving them of a second child so few years after they had lost their first. But I believed Indianapolis was "Indian-no-place," and I was eager to head west.

Fabulous weather, sun-sparkling ocean, palm trees, pastel homes, bright flower beds, and, most of all, the informal life style attracted me. What a contrast to plain Indianapolis of forty years ago! And I could not forget that Doris had encouraged me to make the move. I knew that if I was in California, I would have a chance to get to know this woman I admired, and I set out to do just that.

I returned to work at the newspaper, loaded with stories and photos. Word spread quickly, and a million questions came about my trip to Hollywood: "How did you do it?" "How did you ever get to see Doris Day and have breakfast with her?" "What is she like?" I replied to all, "Oh, it was easy. Doris is a very warm, wonderful, and down-to-earth lady. She made it easy to be a fan."

I went back to writing human-interest stories on a variety of topics from volunteering to fashion shows for charity events, but my heart remained in the Golden State. Mary and I made plans to get an apartment together, with her father in favor. My parents were not. Never mind. The Day Gang was to be my new family, and I looked forward to heading to where the sun sets last in America, and to the sunrise of a new life.

Here I am on the "Bourbon Beat" one Saturday night for The Indianapolis News *in 1967.*

I interviewed Herman from "The Munsters."

Sonny and Cher Bono posed with me at the Coliseum at the Indiana State Fairgrounds. They were part of my "beat" at the Indianapolis News.

Life gets brighter: Doris Day looked like this the day I meet her in 1967.

With her trademark cap, Doris poses with me and an Australian fan.

Grauman's Chinese Theatre's gallery of stars' feet and hands.

4

Moving to Los Angeles and Getting to Know Doris

I could not "go west" immediately because I had to have a job firmly in place. I loved these last days as a reporter at *The News,* a sort of valedictory period. I found a sense of independence in journalism and wrote of kids getting ready for Halloween, the carousel of people at Weir Cook Airport, an English exchange student waiting for first snow, Valentine customs, and opening day at the zoo.

But from Indiana I eagerly pursued employment in California. I was not as adventurous as Eileen had been in just picking up and moving. In January, 1968, before I left, I sent out many letters with my resume, requesting interviews. I wrote to studios, newspapers, and public relations firms. I even got the courage to write to Marty Melcher. This was his reply:

> Dear Mary Anne:
> As per your note of January 30th, I'm sorry to advise that we have no opening in our company. However, I would be happy to sit down with you when you do arrive, to see if I can assist you in any way. Please call my secretary, Phyllis, for an appointment.
> Sincerely yours,
> MARTIN MELCHER

Though I was pleased he was taking interest in my future, I still needed something definite before I made the move. I flew out, and once again

Eileen and Hilda let me spend the week while I went to thirty interviews. I narrowed it down to three offers and finally accepted a position as Assistant Public Relations Director for the May Company in downtown Los Angeles.

During this interview week Mary and I decided to be roommates. She had just graduated from high school and worked for a law firm, and we enjoyed each other's company. We planned to look for an apartment as soon as I moved, but in the meantime we stayed at her uncle's motel.

After my return, my parents said goodbye and gave me their 1965 Dodge GT to make the trip. Uneasy about making the drive alone, I asked a friend with whom I had worked at the department store to go with me.

I began my new job at the May Company on April Fool's Day, 1968, and quit in December on Friday the 13th of the same year. We had a small office with my boss and a secretary. The corporate office exerted almost complete control and stifled our creativity, leaving us feeling smothered if we tried new or creative ideas for clients. The job proved to be a disaster.

Less than a month after I moved, Marty Melcher died on April 20, 1968, of heart failure. We wondered what Doris would do with her husband and manager gone. Through later association with Doris, I learned that Marty was a Jew who turned to the Christian Science faith years before to please Doris, who began following Mary Baker Eddy's teachings while married to her second husband, George Weidler. Toward the end of filming her 39th and final film, *With Six You Get Eggroll,* an Arwin Film Production, in 1968, Marty began to lose weight and took to his bed. He stayed there for three months as Doris nursed him around the clock. Because he rigidly adhered to his view of Christian Science, he insisted that no doctors be called, only his Christian Science Practitioner, Martin Broones, husband of the comic star of vaudeville, radio, and film, Charlotte Greenwood. Broones phoned daily to tell Marty what pages and lines of *Science and Health* by Mrs. Eddy to study and pray with.

Marty developed a real dependence on Doris, and his health continued to decline. Finally, Terry, Doris's son from her first marriage adopted by Marty, brought in Dick Dorso, a friend and partner of Marty's, who persuaded him to allow a physician to see him. They learned that Marty suffered from an enlarged heart, a condition he had apparently lived with for a long time. A specialist ordered him to the hospital immediately. He refused to go by ambulance and was driven to Mount Sinai Hospital, where Doris kept vigil every day from 8:00 AM to midnight. His condition never improved, and early one morning, Doris was called to the hospital. Marty had fallen out of a chair and passed into a coma and underwent emergency surgery. Terry stayed with his mother during the whole ordeal and finally insisted she go home, much against her will. The next morning at 4:00 AM, the hospital called to say that Marty died at age 52.

Marty had signed her to a five-year TV contract to do "The Doris Day Show" for CBS. Floored when she learned this, she eventually realized it saved her emotionally and financially. Working left her no time to feel sorry for herself. Many co-workers on the show were people she had known from the movies. Barbie Lampson, her hairdresser for many years, would be with her, as would Connie Edney, the long-time wardrobe lady on whom Doris relied to select her outfits. Her crew provided a wonderful support system, so in a way Marty's "surprise" proved a blessing in disguise.

It was a while before we saw Doris again, as she passed through the grieving period. We were anxious to express our love and sympathy and to let her know that, even though just fans, we cared. Since we lived less than a mile away, Mary and I often drove past her home. One Friday night after Mary, Eileen, Hilda, and I went to dinner on La Cienega Boulevard, we decided to take one last cruise down Crescent Drive. We noticed activity—people loading up her black station wagon, but we couldn't tell who it was since it was almost dark. We made a u-turn up the street and circled around slowly. Next we saw the headlights heading toward the street and turning left to go to Sunset Boulevard.

We could see Doris in the back with Terry driving and Candy Bergen in the front with him. They lived together at that time. Going on 9:00 PM we were determined to "follow that car," staying far enough back that no one would see us. Two hours later we ended up in Palm Springs. They turned off into a suburban neighborhood and drove directly to a beautiful home on a corner. Once we saw them parked and into the house, we had to find a place to sleep. We were too tired to make the two-hour trip back to LA.

Among us we only had about $5.00, since we had gone to dinner earlier and had not planned on going out of town that night. No one had charge cards back then, relying on a card only for gasoline, so we hoped to find some understanding person who would let us spend the night for $5.00, although that left nothing for food the next morning. Fortunately, we stopped at a small motel in town, and an elderly lady took pity on us and gave us a room. What a break, and they had snacks and fruit in the lobby, so we survived our unplanned trip to Palm Springs.

When we got up the next morning, we noticed bike rentals and many people riding. What a great idea, we thought. Why not go home, return tomorrow, Sunday, with money and more time, rent bikes and ride past the home where Doris, Terry, and Candy were staying? Early Sunday morning four of us started our "pilgrimage" back to Palm Springs. We found a rental place on the main street and gladly paid the day-long fee. We weren't too far from where Doris stayed just off the main street a couple blocks.

The four of us rode around the neighborhood on that sunny Sunday afternoon. We had all biked around the block and approached her home when we noticed a tandem bike with Terry and Candy in the front seat and Doris in the back. My friends looked as though they had seen phantoms. They feared Doris would recognize them and be upset that they were following, or in today's lingo, "stalking" her. She knew their faces, but wouldn't recognize mine because I had only seen her a couple of times. Eileen turned on a dime and headed away, and Hilda and Mary ditched into some bushes as I kept riding. Doris seemed to be wearing a terry robe and held her head down, holding a Kleenex. It was obvious Terry and Candy wanted to get her away from her house.

After they passed, the thrill was gone, and we didn't want her to be upset with us, so we headed back and turned in the bikes. We returned to LA on the freeway about 4:00 PM. Eileen drove and spotted a custom car with Tennessee plates. She said, "That has to be Elvis Presley's car," and, sure enough, it was. Eileen quickly maneuvered her car next to his on the passenger side. There was the king, Elvis in living color, wearing a red sweater, looking very tan, his black hair slicked into place, chatting with the other passengers and puffing on a cigar. We rolled down our windows, and he did the same. For nearly two hours as we drove side by side, he talked to us, blowing smoke rings out the window and saying things like, "I wish I had known you girls were in Palm Springs." We filmed him with our super-8 movie cameras. What I wouldn't have given for a video recorder with sound back then! We wondered what exit he would use; he got off at Robertson Boulevard, the one we used as we lived one block east on Olympic Boulevard. That was quite a weekend—going to Palm Springs with Doris Day and returning to the city with Elvis!

Mary and I enjoyed our apartment just one block from Beverly Hills, and it cost just $125 a month, amazing when one compares it to today's rent schedules. Our managers, Mr. and Mrs. Axtell, a gracious couple who lived in Culver City, were generous to their two renters. Mary's father lived less than a mile from us and often came loaded down with groceries or took us out for dinner. We also cooked for him on occasion, and he enjoyed that.

Time passed, and Doris would soon be getting over her mourning. We either rode our bikes or drove to Bailey's Bakery, hoping to meet her on Saturday mornings. She didn't seem to mind that we would show up around the same time as she, but we again feared she would think we stalked her. The thrill of the chase drove us to want a glimpse of our heroine. Beyond that, we loved Doris and wanted her to know us as friends and supporters. Mary was no stranger to her; they had met many times either by her home or at a Dodgers or Lakers game. I was the newcomer—but not for long.

Doris had to know we were coming for her because we never saw any other young people hanging out there, nor were there autograph seekers around. She may have felt flattered that we would seek her out, and gradually she felt at home with us and seemed to enjoy the company of our group, young enough to be her daughters, innocent and non-threatening. Her own son was two years older than I!

One Sunday morning Mary and I wore our bathing suits driving to the beach, taking Sunset Boulevard, and as we drove by Doris's home, we saw her black station wagon pull out of the driveway. I was driving and decided to go around the block and follow. Doris and her mother Alma headed for Nate 'N Al's, the popular restaurant in Beverly Hills where many show people ate. We watched as her car slowed up to let her mother out. I eased past to a parking place up the street. Mary and I sat watching as Doris pulled up beside us and started to park in a place just behind my car. We figured we should get out because it would look strange if we just sat there and she recognized us.

Mary jumped out first, caught Doris's eye, and called to her. I started to get out; I could hear Doris calling back to Mary. It sounded as if she wanted to talk, and I was excited. She wanted to talk all right! Still seated in the car, she leaned out her window repeating, "Were you following me?" We were speechless. She didn't like people to follow her. If we really were her friends, we would not do that. We were guilty, and she knew it. Meekly, we promised never to follow again. I could well understand her feelings, especially with Marty gone. Selfish, unable to put ourselves in Doris's place, a recent widow with fans, we were indeed—I hate to use the term—"gently stalking" her. True, she was a public figure. Also true, that we were young and a little immature. Still, Mary and I regretted causing her to be so unsettled. She lived in a fish bowl, and we had our noses pressed up to the glass.

Our "legitimate" meeting ground, which Doris seemed to encourage, was Bailey's. Mary and I looked forward to our Saturday mornings with the chance that we would see Doris. We were always welcomed by the friendly older lady, Hilda Turner, the manager, who treated us like daughters.

In the spirit of not bothering Doris when she appeared, we let her speak first. Hilda confided that sometimes, depending on the star's mood, she might not be fond of our popping in at the same time as she. However, Hilda reminded Doris that this was a public place, with "the girls" as welcome as any other paying customer. We attributed Doris's hesitation about our coming in as an indication she was still getting over Marty's death. Most of the time, though, she remained her old effervescent self. As time went on, she seemed to look forward to seeing us. Mary and I gradually moved up the fan ladder with the ultimate goal of being Doris Day's welcomed acquaintances. She was easy to know, open and confiding. The more Doris got to know us, the more comfortable she became, often sharing thoughts about her mother and her work or about decorating her home.

Doris had begun the TV show in June of 1968, and we always commented on the past week's show. She seemed eager to hear our reactions and often told stories about what went on at the set. She talked about the show on which Billy De Wolfe appeared as guest star, playing her neighbor, Mr. Jarvis. Billy always made her laugh. She spoke of his love for her little Muffy, a chocolate-brown poodle, whom he affectionately called his "Myra." Doris used to get upset with CBS when they pre-empted her show for some sports event—and especially for all the NASA coverage during those days when the astronauts first went into space. We sympathized. It wasn't fair; all the major events took place on Tuesday nights in her time slot between 9:30 PM and 10:00 PM.

Eventually Doris began bringing her mother and her Aunt Marie, whom she lovingly called "Rocky," to the bakery. Rocky, the lady who sent me the fan photos, had moved from Cincinnati to live with Doris, a big adjustment for her, and Doris did all she could to make her feel at home.

During those months in 1969 when Doris filmed "The Doris Day Show" between June and December, we saw more of Alma and Rocky than the TV star herself. Doris was often too tired on Saturdays to get up early to go to Bailey's. While she was filming, she got up about 5:30 AM and was picked up by her driver, Del Brown, around 6:30 AM to make the drive over Coldwater Canyon, arriving at CBS Studio Center for a 7:00 AM call. Despite the great difference in our ages, (50 years at least) Rocky, Alma, Mary, and I got along well. Mary tended to be with Alma, and I chatted with Rocky, and we looked forward to our times with them. This pattern continued for months, but every once in a while Doris would join us.

That year we woke up one Sunday morning to the tragic news that actress Sharon Tate, along with others, had been murdered at the Polanski home on Cielo Drive. The address sounded vaguely familiar to me, and then I remembered hearing Doris talking about going on occasion to see her son at a Cielo Drive address when he had been with Candy Bergen. Terry and Candy had lived there for some time, but had recently moved to Doris's beach home. Horrific details began to surface.

Terry's name came up in the reports because Charles Manson had been briefly associated with him. Manson had believed Terry would foster his musical aspirations, but when this failed to happen, he grew infuriated, feeling betrayed. He had apparently been to the Cielo Drive address, and although he knew Melcher had moved, the house and the neighborhood apparently represented his rejection by the show business establishment. Manson believed he could instigate a race war by having his followers slaughter wealthy people in their homes and cast suspicion on black militant groups such as the Black Panthers. He instructed Tex Watson, Susan Atkins, Pat Krenwinkel, Leslie Van Houton, and Linda Kasabian to complete the atrocities, killing innocent victims by slitting their throats in Sharon and Roman Polanski's home, the recent former home of Doris's son.

What must have been going through Doris's mind as the details of this horrendous "Helter Skelter" night unfolded? We prayed for her and Terry. We didn't see much of Doris for a couple of weeks. She was not at Bailey's when we were, but Hilda told us she had spoken to her. How would all these horrible crimes in her son's former home impact her, right in the middle of filming her series? Then one day after riding our bikes to Bailey's, we found Doris. She spoke candidly about the whole ordeal, and there was a somber mood at the bakery.

You could sense that she was relieved Terry no longer lived at that home, but you could also see the concern for him now that his name came up prominently in the news media. He would have to testify. Soon grim pictures of him leaving the court room appeared in newspapers and on TV. The whole city of Los Angeles mourned, because not only did they have to deal with the Tate murders, but also the night following that killing orgy, grocery chain owner, Leno LaBianca and his wife Rosemary had been murdered by the Manson family in their Los Feliz home. When the Manson clan were tried, convicted, and sentenced to life prison terms, the city breathed a sigh of relief.

At least once a year, Alma would go to Houston to visit her daughter-in-law Shirley and her grandchildren. Shirley had been married to Doris's older brother Paul, who died in the late 1950s in a baseball accident. "Mom" looked forward to these trips and always came home with stories about the family. One Friday evening after Alma left town, the phone rang at our apartment. I answered, and it was Doris! I listened intently as she talked. She told me that Alma would be gone for a couple of weeks. She wanted some things from Farmer's Market and wondered if we would meet her there to shop. I was excited; Mary stood by me almost yanking the phone away. Doris suggested we meet at the little restaurant at the market for breakfast and then do her shopping.

Ordinarily, Alma did a lot of the shopping for Doris, and a favorite place to buy was the famous Farmer's Market a couple miles from her home, where everything was very fresh. Fanatical about food, Doris loved broccoli and green beans and good cuts of meat. Mary and I had gone with Alma a couple of times and helped her carry the packages. That whole night I doubt I had much, if any, sleep. Doris had called us and asked us to go with her. Previously, we were fortunate to just be at Bailey's the same time as she was with nothing planned in advance. This was definitely a BIG step in our relationship. We had moved from support to companionship, or close to it. And I could always hope for "friend."

Believing Doris should not have to wait for us, we scrambled to get ready in the morning to be on time. We arrived at the restaurant about 9:00 AM and Doris came in shortly thereafter. She had her usual: eggs over easy, wheat toast, crisp bacon, coffee, and orange juice. Our hearts pounded. There we sat at breakfast with one of the biggest stars in the world, and she had done the inviting.

Doris told us her mother had called to report on the family. After breakfast, she paid, and we walked through the parking lot to the center of the market. Doris, a good shopper, knew exactly what she wanted, the quality of meat and so forth. Because she had donned her floppy hat and sun glasses, not many people recognized her. We stayed close to carry purchases and help in any way we could as she went to a few vendors. She purchased fruits, vegetables, and small beef filets. She was a queen; Mary and I, her ladies-in-waiting. I couldn't wait to tell my parents and some of my close friends in Indianapolis.

Doris gets ready to bike down to Bailey's Bakery.

But who's the gal in the striped t-shirt? Doris loved to cruise the sidewalks and streets on a regular basis and visit with friends, including some of her fans.

On a more somber note, Terry Melcher emerges as a witness from the Manson trial.

The Los Angeles Times

5

My Dream Job by Accident

After leaving the May Company in December, 1968, I had gone to work for the Cintel Corporation in West Los Angeles, about a 15-minute drive from my home. I assisted the publications manager, a Mr. Beachley. The company made manuals for the US Air Force during this period of the Vietnam War. Although it was not my area of expertise, which was public relations, we were quite busy, and I enjoyed my tasks and co-workers.

Mary and I remained on the lookout for Doris Day movies, checking the guide in the newspaper weekly. The *LA Times* calendar section informed us that Doris's 1968 MGM movie, *Where Were You When The Lights Went Out?* co-starring Patrick O'Neal, ran in Long Beach for a week. After work on Friday, June 26, 1970, we drove the San Diego Freeway in rush-hour traffic to Long Beach to have a brief visit with Mary's mom and two brothers before going to the movie.

On the night we arrived, her older brother was moving out of town. Because the house was filled with well-wishers, we ducked out to get to the theater by show time. Once the movie was over, we drove to her mother's home before making the trip back to Los Angeles. I spent a few minutes with Mary's other brother, just returned from the Vietnam War a month before. He was a very nice man, and we had dated and had good times together. Since the house was still full of friends, the younger brother asked me to go outside so we could talk. We sat in his month-old car, a shiny, new green

TR-6 he had special-ordered from Germany. He was so proud of that car.

We decided to drive to a corner restaurant for a drink. He seemed to me to have had some drinks before we arrived. I had only one drink and wanted to get back to LA. We left the restaurant about midnight for his mother's home. I didn't know Long Beach well and in the dark was not at all familiar with the neighborhoods. All I remember was riding in the swerving car. The next thing I recall is being in the emergency room at Long Beach Community Hospital with someone asking me to remove my contact lenses. We had been in a serious accident, and I was lucky to be alive.

My friends delivered the dreaded phone message to my parents. I knew this would upset them, as it was a vivid reminder of the call about my brother John's fatal car accident in 1963. But I could at least tell them my situation. I wouldn't die. The accident happened on their 28th wedding anniversary in 1970. I had two broken legs, with my right arm sustaining a fracture and dislocation of the right talus. My right eyelid was slashed, with a lot of glass embedded in my face from the windshield. Fortunately I had no internal injuries, and the bones would eventually heal. My forehead required plastic surgery, and I had skillful and dedicated doctors during my 19 days in the hospital.

My Day Gang friends, Eileen, Hilda, and Lauren, came to visit me as often as possible. The visitors whom I most appreciated were Mr. and Mrs. Beachley, my boss and his wife, who drove in every night from their home in Manhattan Beach, at least a thirty-minute drive. Maybe Beachley felt sorry for me after I asked Mary to call him that Saturday morning, so I could tell him from my hospital bed, as I awaited surgery, that I would not be able to work the following Monday and that I was not sure when I would be back.

In no time Mary got word to Doris, her mom, and Rocky. While I was in the hospital, Doris sent me a candygram, telling me she hoped I would be up and out soon, signed, "Much love, Doris!" Alma sent me cards and letters. In her first one she wrote:

> Hi, Sweetie Think of you everyday and remember you in my prayers. I went up to the coffee shop and felt real bad about your terrible accident. It seems the innocent get the bad breaks...time will fly and you will be your same sweet self...Bye Dear...be a good girl.
> Love, Alma

It was comforting to know Doris and Alma cared. Laughingly I told myself they were involved. After all, if not such a Day fan, I would not have gone to Long Beach to see her movie.

When confined to a hospital bed, you begin to recognize people's walk and the sound of feet. The first two weeks I was pretty weak, and as much as I appreciated a visit, I would have preferred to rest. It became a chore to stay focused and up for conversations, but I gradually grew stronger. And as much as I had dreaded being in a hospital, when I was to be released, I cried. Everyone had been so good to me, so solicitous and helpful.

I was to be in a wheelchair for six months. Mary quit her job to take care of me. Tired, I rested a lot. When I finally ventured out of our second floor apartment, I managed to scoot down the stairs sitting, flopping and taking them one by one. Mary lugged my wheelchair up and down and stationed it at the bottom. With a little ingenuity and a lot of courage, we got through, and I determined not to be confined to four walls even though confined to two wheels.

I will always remember that very first day I ventured out. Friends had stopped in one Sunday afternoon. They helped me get down the stairs one by one. One had a pillow under my arm and another under my legs, and I held onto the railing with my left arm, a real logistical problem, but we were doing pretty well. When we got to the last step, I could see a lady in a light blue dress approaching—Alma Day.

"What are you trying to do? You better get back up those stairs," she said emphatically. I tried to explain that I just had to get out, and since I had help, I was going to try. My comments fell on deaf ears, and she pointed her finger at me. All of a sudden, I was on my way back up with Alma supervising the whole mission. She confided that this brought back memories of the time she broke her leg in New York City, and she wanted me to take no chances. A couple of days went by when I received the following note:

> Dear Mary Anne, Do hope you are on the mend and please don't go down the steps until you move down there. I think about you and remember you in my prayers. I just can't believe that you have so much will power and do so many things for yourself. You are such a sweet girl and oh, how sad, when I heard this sad news about your accident... be a good girl and no steps or I will spank your little ass, ha, ha.
> Lots of love, ALMA

In a few weeks Mary and I became pros in getting me up and down that flight of stairs safely. Eventually, I maneuvered into a car. Mary packed my wheelchair in the trunk, and we headed for Bailey's. Doris autographed my casts, which changed frequently over the months. She always had something new to write. One saying was, "The best is yet to come," a favorite saying of hers and my motto ever since. Mary and I began meeting Alma and Rocky again at a new place, Martha Randall's Coffee Shop, on Beverly Drive across from Nate 'N Al's famous deli. Hilda Turner had left Bailey's and now worked here; so we followed. When we got together, Mary listened to Alma, and I resumed conversations with Rocky, often talking about Cincinnati.

One evening we received a call from Aunt Rocky to see how I was feeling. She said she was lonely and missed her Ohio friends. I knew about her loneliness from our talks and felt sorry for her. Doris tried to do all she could, but sometimes Rocky seemed a fish out of water, even though she was with family. Other times, she seemed quite content. It must have been hard for a lady in her 70s to be transplanted from the Midwest, where her friends lived, to Beverly Hills. Rocky told me she enjoyed being around younger people, but hesitated, since Alma told her "not to get too close." Her comment left me bewildered.

One morning when Mary and I ate at Randall's, Doris came in and sat with us. Seeing me in my wheelchair, she began to talk about a train accident when she was in her early teens. She made a point of showing me that a scar on her leg was almost non-existent, comforting me because I still had scars that showed. When we left, she pushed my wheelchair up and down Beverly Drive, a ride I'll always remember.

After six long months in a wheelchair and several casts later, I graduated to crutches. It was a blessing to be able to navigate on my own and with just one cast left on my right leg, so driving was no problem. Mary went back to work with my deep gratitude. What a devoted friend she had been through all of this—a true life-saver for me, physically, mentally, and emotionally! I never got depressed or bored, taking up painting little wooden plaques with a "Flavia"-type character. They became my Christmas gifts that year, and I painted one for Doris with daisies on it. She wrote me a sweet note saying she loved it and hung it in her bathroom off her bedroom.

I had told my parents that as soon as I could walk, I would return for a couple months, so I flew home for the Christmas holidays. I spent a great deal of time with my father, now retired. While in Indianapolis I received two beautiful letters from Doris, and my dad was happy Doris wrote. Having friends in for lunch, he proudly commented, "Mary Anne has had two personal letters from Doris Day since she's been home." He had a special gleam in his eyes as he played the role of boastful father. He rarely said anything about Doris, but I know this time he rejoiced with me, in spite of groaning so often about it while I was in school.

The first letter told me she was pleased I was getting around on crutches and encouraged me to keep up the good work, "and it won't be long and you'll be working again and really enjoy yourself." She wrote she didn't think I'd be able to resist California forever and wished me a beautiful Christmas.

The second letter came following Aunt Marie's (Rocky's) death.

> Yes, it was a very strange Christmas for us here, but I want you to know that all is well and Nana and I are both fine. It's really strange without Rocky but I must tell you that she is closer than ever before to me. I feel no sense of separation whatsoever.

Rocky had died on Christmas day that year, and my Aunt Marie died in late January. Doris and I suffered the loss of a loved one within days of one another, both ironically with the same name.

In late January I returned to Los Angeles and started back to trying to improve, getting out for breakfast occasionally. I still had months of recuperation and more surgery to remove the pins from my ankle and right arm, depending on how quickly the bones mended. I had wonderful doctors working with me. Mary's mother made sure I had the best. Fortunately, I had long-term disability through my work at the Cintel Corporation, because a great deal of time went by as I progressed.

After I resumed going to breakfast regularly, I found Doris was on hiatus from filming her TV series and not due to start filming again until June. When the two of us began meeting in the mornings at Randall's, we got into some great conversations. She began talking to me about religion, revealing some of her philosophy. She spoke a lot about Joel Goldsmith, a teacher and metaphysician, and about his book, *The Infinite Way,* her favorite of his works. She said, "Just put it in your desk and open it whenever. Then what I do, in front there will be certain messages that would concern my work, and I'll mark a page with 'good for work' or 'good for Terry.' Then

I'll read something for him. But I have everything marked. It should really be indexed. I ruin my books because I mark them all up. I use a red pencil, or blue or something, and when you find a passage that's really great, I underline and underline all the words."

I know she took spirituality seriously. Doris still felt strongly about some Christian Science beliefs, although she visited physicians when she felt she needed to. She read Mary Baker Eddy's book and had a copy handy at all times. After second husband George Wielder introduced her to Christian Science, she followed it seriously for several years. She loved much of the overall theology of the religion.

Suddenly, she looked up and asked, "What time does the Food Giant open? I have to get hot dogs for the dogs. I don't give them many, but every other morning I give them bite-size pieces, and do they love it! When I open my refrigerator, they know what's coming." Off she flew to the grocery, and I was off to read the spiritual books she gave me.

Each day our conversation varied, but somehow we always came back to religion. I found it most interesting to talk to Doris about this because we were both raised in the Catholic faith, but had gone in our own directions. Doris got me thinking for myself, and by reading the Goldsmith books I became aware of her views. It was fascinating, and I always enjoyed our conversations and learned so much from her. She said, "Death is a higher level of life." The more she talked, the more I began to think, and the more interested I became in learning her views. Eventually she gave me an inscribed copy of *Science and Health*.

I had a whole new sense of awareness. Little did we know she was preparing me for a traumatic event. With her help, understanding, and guidance, I was able to deal with the fact that my father was very ill following several heart attacks. My mother called, and I flew to Chicago where he lay dying. She and I spent the month of May in the waiting room off the cardiac unit at Billings Hospital at Chicago University. The doctors advised us not to take a hotel room, but to be near. The nurses made us as comfortable as possible in the waiting room just seconds from his bedside. Still on crutches, I hobbled around that huge hospital as best I could to keep up with my mother.

My father had become too weak to have surgery, and things looked bad. Doris wrote me several notes of encouragement. In one she reminded me, "All *is* well, isn't it?" She told me to "Use what you know. It really works." She told me she believed I would have the strength I needed to face losing my dad. "Put your hand in *His*," she urged.

I returned to Los Angeles briefly for a doctor's appointment and attended the Motion Picture Mother's Association luncheon at the Beverly Hills Hotel with Doris, her mom, Connie Edney, her wardrobe lady and friend for many years, and Mary as Doris's guests. We had a great time, and for a few moments, it took my mind off my sadness. Everyone treated me kindly, and I was grateful to Doris for going out of her way to help me. On May 29, 1971, I received the call from my mother that all efforts failed, and my dad had passed away. I flew to Indianapolis immediately to be with her and my family. I know that if Doris had not prepared me for this experience in her own sweet and loving way, I would have gone to pieces. As a result, I could help my mother through the weeks ahead, staying with her for two months and then returning to Los Angeles.

One morning when just Doris and I were having breakfast at Randall's, a girl came in. She seemed nervous, but Doris called out to her, and she came over to our table. "Doris, I didn't want to bother you, but I made this for you and saw your bike and knew you must be inside," she said sheepishly. Doris introduced me to Linda Cowan, daughter of Warren Cowan of Rogers and Cowan, Doris's long-time publicity agent and friend. We didn't say much; Linda was not at ease and said she had to get to work and was running late. She gave Doris a beautiful small painting, and Doris loved it.

Once Linda left, Doris proceeded to tell me that Linda's parents were good friends, and she and Marty had done a lot of things with the couple years before when the kids, including Terry, were much younger. The Cowans befriended the Melchers early in Doris's career, and the two couples and their three children enjoyed many trips together to Lake Arrowhead. Linda used to say Doris watched her grow up.

In the next few weeks, Linda would pop in to say "Hi" on her way to work and visited with Doris and me for a few minutes each time. Doris thought that it would be nice if Mary and I and Linda got to know one another, so the next time Linda dropped in, we exchanged phone numbers, and, after that, our friendship and mutual admiration for Doris grew. I was eager to hear the stories Linda could tell, since she had known the Melchers for many years. She joined our circle of fan friends. Linda seemed pleased to find others who shared her love for Doris. She had a younger sister who recently had married and lived a more conventional lifestyle than Linda's.

Despite her "Hollywood" heritage as the daughter of an influential man who represented the cream of the industry, Linda seemed insecure, especially around Doris, whom she had known since she was a toddler. Linda's mom Ronnie had divorced Warren several years before and moved to London where she was a writer. Linda's father married actress Barbara Rush and lived two blocks from Doris. So our circle expanded.

When Doris and I met for breakfast during this period, we talked about many things. She was a great conversationalist, and I listened intently to every word. It was as though she was my teacher, and in a way she was. She spoke often about Dr. Robert Schuller, the "Hour of Power" minister from Garden Grove, California, although these conversations took place sometime in 1971 before the building of the Crystal Cathedral.

Even though Doris didn't go to any church, she had a wide-ranging faith and watched his "Hour of Power" every week. She and Dr. Schuller had become great friends and talked frequently on the phone. Mary and I wanted to see this famous minister and his church, so Doris made arrangements. Driving to Garden Grove, we attended his service and were escorted up the elevator to his office with a panoramic view. Dr. Schuller was gracious to us and spoke highly of Doris. After we visited about a half hour, we thanked him. He cordially showed us around the building, telling us about his dream for a church of glass with gardens and many ministries. The following Saturday when we saw Doris at Randall's, she wanted to know all about our visit. You could sense she would have loved to go with us. She told us her friend, Billy De Wolfe, wanted to go, too, and one day he would take her.

I was still "crippling" around all this time, almost a year since my accident, and Doris knew I had weeks of healing and waiting for the operation to remove the pins. We continued our daily visits, and she encouraged me to make use of my remaining free time. She suggested I take a course in shorthand and mentioned the possibility of working at the studio. I didn't know what was in her mind, but I took the opportunity to improve my business skills. I found Willis Business College in Santa Monica and signed up for a ten-week, speed-writing class that met five days a week for five hours daily. I was determined to master secretarial skills.

The following day I met Doris at the bakery and told her that I took her advice and signed up for a speed-writing course. Doris turned to Hilda and said, "She's going to take speed-writing. Terrific!" I added, "If I don't learn it this time, I never will." Doris leaned over to me and said, "You know, you're bright, and you'll learn fast. She'd make a great secretary, yes, she would."

Then she paused. The subject seemed to fascinate her. She said, "It doesn't seem like it would be too difficult. Learning speed-writing shouldn't take very long at that rate. It's just shorthand and is really interesting, I think. I would like to know how to take shorthand. Listen, will you tell me why they don't teach that in high school?'

"They do," I replied.

"Really?" It had been a while since she had been in high school, I guess.

I recalled that my mother could do shorthand in her sleep and never could understand why I couldn't pick it up. I had taken a class years before in Indianapolis at Broad Ripple High School as an extra evening class, but it was once a week for three hours, and during the week it was not always convenient to keep up, so I never mastered the skill. Now with going Monday through Friday for ten weeks, you had to keep up; otherwise, you might as well throw your money away.

I brought my tape recorder and taped each speed-writing class, playing it back over and over in the afternoon and evening. I had little or no social life, as I wanted to master this class and be able to report good news back to Doris. As weeks passed, I made sure Doris knew of my progress because she seemed genuinely interested. The 10 weeks seemed to go by quickly, and I passed with flying colors. You-know-who was the first to know! She was delighted and congratulated me on my effort.

Now that I could maneuver on my own, Mary took a vacation with her family to Hawaii for two weeks, and Doris invited Linda and me to her home. I used a cane, hobbling around. Doris greeted us at the door, and as a fan I was struck dumb. Being with her at the restaurant was meaningful, but being at her home was extraordinary. I wished I had brought my camera. The thing I remember most was the aroma of eucalyptus drifting through the house. Her living room was inviting, and when you walked in the front door, you could see directly through it and out to her brick patio with white wicker furniture and then on to the swimming pool. Arrangements of daisies abounded.

Her home was decorated in what I would call country antique. The furniture did not have the austere feel the furniture in many Beverly Hills homes had. The carpeting in the large L-shaped living room was a golden shag that complemented the rust-colored sectional sofa in the main room. A baby grand piano stood in one part of the living room near the fireplace. The view of her patio, swimming pool, and spacious back yard invited the visitor to step outside. You could see a giant sycamore tree jutting out of the bricked patio that led to the pool, overshadowing the house and patio. She commented that the old tree was one of the selling points when she and Marty purchased the home in 1957.

Even though Linda had known Doris for years, it had been a long time since she had been at her home, and the two of us looked and listened as Doris took us on a mini-tour. Many well behaved dogs came to greet us, soon quieting down on the cushions of the sofa and chairs. Linda shared my love of animals, and we played with Doris's shaggy friends for a while. "I'm just a boarder in a dog house," Doris said laughingly. She called her home the "Canine Country Club." It was just that. Anyone who passed through her gates and got a glimpse of the "dog's life" her pooches enjoyed might vow to be reincarnated as one of them. As she said, "These kids have it made, they know it, and believe me, they run the show!" As excited as I was about being there, the question crossed my mind, "What am I going to tell Mary when she comes back?" She would feel left out. She had so hoped for a visit.

Alma's birthday was July 6th, with Doris eager to do something special for her. Since she was working on the TV set, she decided to do a surprise party. She planned to invite several of Alma's friends, including Olive Abbott, sister of veteran actor Bud Abbott, and two former housekeepers who were like family, Kay Bowker, nearly 90 years old and Katie Mattox, in her late 70s. These two had all but raised Terry during the many years Doris's career was developing. Billy De Wolfe, executive producer Don Genson, and Ruth Williams, another friend of Doris's and Alma's, Mary, Linda, and I were also invited. I had the temerity to believe we were being considered as equals and friends.

The party was planned to be a surprise for Alma, and it turned out that way. The guests arrived early, assembling in Doris's "living room" on the set. Balloons, flowers, and well-wishers contributed to the festive feeling. Doris had ordered an artistically decorated cake as well as snacks. She filmed that day, and her "dress" for the scene was the costume of a French waitress, complete with the stereotypical black dress and white lacy apron. In between shots she ran into the dressing room to make sure everything would be in place for the guests. At the designated time, there was a knock at the door, and we all became very quiet. The door opened and Alma appeared, as we burst into "Happy Birthday."

Alma was happy to see Katie and Kay, greeting them warmly, and after all the hugging and kissing, she began opening gifts. An unusual one was the one presented by Linda, an artist with a unique sense of humor. One of Alma's favorite sayings when talking about a real jerk was labeling them a member of the "Flying Ass Hole Club!" Linda was creative with a Styrofoam ball on a wire, attaching feathers as wings on either side and putting markings to make it look like that orifice in flight. It brought much laughter. Mary, Linda, and I were pleased to be a part of the celebration and took everything in. The housekeepers, Katie and Kay, whom we had heard so much about from both Doris and Alma, had been faithful to Doris all these years and felt honored to be included in the celebration. I took several photos of Doris and Alma with her guests and made arrangements to send everybody copies.

At long last the date came to remove the pins. I returned to Long Beach Community Hospital because my doctor was on staff there and I trusted him. The surgery proved to be a breeze—in one day and out the next. Everything had mended as it should, with the doctors pleased.

A couple of days before I returned to my job with Cintel Corporation, Doris phoned to ask if I could serve as aide for her at the studio for a few days. Ruth, one of her mother's friends, had been helping on occasion but had to be out of town, leaving Doris without any help with her hectic schedule and her dogs.

We arrived at the CBS lot in Studio City at 7:00 AM and Doris went into make-up. While she was busy filming right outside her dressing room on stages 8 and 9, I had charge of the five dogs she brought to the studio every day: Rudy and Schatzie, two dachshunds, Bucky, a sweet, buck-tooth mix; Little Tiger, a small black poodle; and Muffy, a brown poodle. In addition, I answered the phones and helped the driver fix her lunch or dinner. She had a kitchen, a living-room area, a large dressing room, a full bathroom with shower, and a make-up room just around the corner. Formerly this dressing room had been used by Barbara Stanwyck when CBS filmed her "Big Valley" series. Doris said she completely redid it to suit her taste, homey and inviting.

During one break, Doris decided to see what I had learned at speed-writing school and dictated a couple of letters. She was pleased with the results, and so was I. She knew that I could handle things, but I guess she wanted to make sure and watched my reactions. On the last day Doris gave me a card that simply said, "Thanks. Clara." (Clara was her nickname—more on that later.) A check was also enclosed, which I didn't want to take; however, she insisted.

The following week I returned to Cintel. They had held my position for 14 months during my long-term disability, and I was deeply grateful. Everyone greeted me warmly with a luncheon in my honor. Overwhelmed, I took it in stride and worked to get back into the routine. I typed many letters, which Mr. Beachley dictated to companies we dealt with for supplies and information. Occasionally I helped bind manuals in a large room devoted to this process. The Vietnam War kept us busy cranking out the publications. The work was not creative, but the people were personable, and it delivered a paycheck.

Two days later Doris called me at my office and asked, "Mary Anne, how would you like to come work for me?" I didn't even take a breath and happily answered, "I'd love it, Clara. YES!" We chatted briefly about how soon I could begin. My boss had been so kind over the past 14 months, but I had to tell him I was now going to be Doris Day's personal secretary! Mr. Beachley couldn't have been nicer. When I told him my news, he said that since the Vietnam War was winding down, our company would probably not have that much to do anyway. He knew of my admiration for Doris and with a gleam in his eye wished me well.

After my accident, my cast kept me restricted for several months. Alma Day visited me.

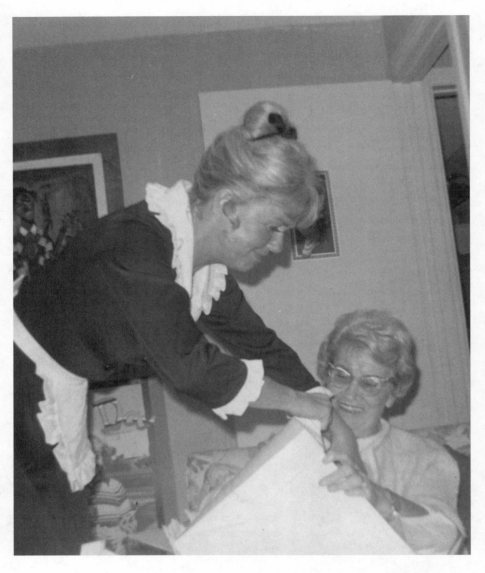

Daughter and mother at the TV studio, a surprise party for Alma's birthday, July 6, 1971. Doris was in the costume of a French maid.

6

No Glamour in Hollywood

Doris Day: a professional perfectionist to the last detail in all phases of filming and in my opinion the greatest actress ever. Perhaps I had surmised that before, but I learned it first hand on my first day on the job. My months of freedom over, I was now Doris's personal secretary and on call all the time. Elation mixed with trepidation in my approach to the job.

I attended Doris the whole time she was at the studio from 7:00 AM to about 7:00 PM to care for the five dogs she brought to the set, to feed them, walk them, and keep them quiet; and to prepare meals for Doris—breakfast, lunch, and dinner, and protein drink in the afternoon. I answered fan mail, made appointments for her, and kept up with correspondence. I tidied her dressing room and assisted her in any other way I could. Just as she had become a lovely acquaintance and friend, she was a lovely person to work for, organized but not demanding.

My mother became the first to know about my new position and to congratulate me. Friends and relatives started calling and sending wires. My alma mater, *The Indianapolis News*, ran the following notice:

> The advice "Go West, young man," didn't turn out too badly for Miss Mary Anne Barothy, formerly a feature writer for the woman's pages of *The Indianapolis News*. She just became personal secretary to movie star, Doris Day. Miss Barothy is the daughter of Mrs. Charles Barothy and the late Mr. Barothy.

All my friends and relatives seemed genuinely pleased that I finally achieved the goal I had set years before.

But if I had sought glamour, it didn't take long to realize there was none left in Hollywood. Maybe it had never been there, only a lot of hard work, long hours, and the need to wear many hats. Each night after a long day of filming, Doris called to me, "Sleep fast, dear," as she rode past in her dark green Imperial. You could see her nestled in the back seat with the little light on, reading the script for the next day, with her dogs still settling. By the time we both reached Coldwater Canyon, all canine heads in the car were down, and you could only catch a glimpse of her shining blond hair under the reading lamp. She knew the drive by heart and never had to look up to know where she was.

Several times I was asked to go to Doris's home and rode with them, usually having little Bubbles, a black schnoodle, or Rudy, the elderly dachshund, in my lap. The other four-leggers found a comfortable spot close to their mom. Doris sometimes used the time to rest, but many times worked on the current script or rewrote it for the following week. She knew instinctively when the wording or action fell below par and would labor hours to get the fine points right. She knew her audience and every angle of filming and made the work look like a snap.

Doris had a talented and professional crew working on her series. Most had significant experience on other top shows: camera men, a greens man, key grip, best-boy, directors, assistant directors, and many others. The directors used three camera angles for every shot, which gave them a variety of shots to choose from before the finished production, just as if filming a movie.

Being the competent artist she was, Doris expected the same work ethic from others. In our "spare" time Doris dictated letters. I typed in my free minutes in my office at one end of her living room in the dressing room apartment. Between scenes she could come in to check on pending matters or make calls. I handled everything from that one location. The other office staff members were located in another building about a block away from the sound stages.

Doris had an ideal setup at CBS with her dressing room right off the two stages where she filmed. Yellows, golds, and whites created a bright and cheerful setting. You could see touches of Doris's own favorite decorative items, with fresh daisies in vases all around. She often used the bath and shower and enjoyed a large dressing room with wall-to-wall mirrors and closets galore, plus a full kitchen. Just outside the living room was her make-up room, decorated in pink and white tones, where she spent many hours in a comfortable chair. Sometimes she would start humming a song and then start singing. I would stop and listen to her, as she sang in a voice as beautiful and strong as it had been during her singing years, and with perfect pitch.

Doris usually arrived with dogs first thing in the morning, wearing a robe and house slippers. She headed right for the make-up room, where she carefully put on her own make-up. She was a master at this. The only assistance she occasionally needed was help in applying her eyelashes. Barbie Lampson, her long-time friend and hairdresser, worked with her hair and took great pains with "old faithful," a small hair piece Doris used to add height. This piece was guarded with everyone's life and treated like a gold bar.

Before Doris made up, she usually put in her breakfast order. I learned exactly how she liked her food. The driver and I rotated around the kitchen and made the most of every minute. She was always hungry in the morning, declaring breakfast her favorite meal. Easy to please, she liked her coffee hot with cream, her soft-boiled eggs on the loose side and accompanied by very crisp bacon, and her toast well done and buttered. I learned how to fry bacon to perfection under driver Del's astute supervision.

One day Doris raved about the Eggs Benedict she had over the weekend at the Beverly Hills Hotel, so Del and I decided to give her a treat. We found a simple recipe for Hollandaise sauce, bought the rest of the fixings, and surprised her with our specialty of the day. She ate it with gusto and voiced her approval for our creation. Another day she had a taste for pancakes, and the "Del and Mary Kitchen" turned out the order of appealing flapjacks with butter and syrup. Doris seemed to like whatever we fixed and went out of her way to say "thank you." She knew, and knows, how to win people over, but her approval reflects genuine interest.

Since I had been there two weeks earlier, I had met some of her co-workers on the set. As I took over the secretary's job, she toured me around to make sure I had been introduced to everyone, telling people I was her first private secretary. Previously she shared a secretary with her husband Marty, but now I was hers exclusively. She seemed gratified to have one person she could count on and did not have to share.

That first day during a break between scenes, she took me on a walk on the back lot with the dogs, who bounded along with her. The popular western "Gunsmoke" was filmed on this back lot, and as we walked down Main Street past the false fronts, she pointed out some of the sights. When we ran into actress Patricia Neal, Doris introduced me, and they chatted briefly.

I'll never forget what Doris told me one day: "People have no idea what I do. Well, you do. There's always somebody pushing, 'Five minutes, ready when you are.' 'We have five minutes of lighting, and then we are ready for you.' All day long I hear this. Is it any wonder my stomach is in knots? Yet it is enjoyable. It would be marvelous if you could do twelve shows and then take off. You just can't do that because you would lose your crew." What she meant is that they needed to film twenty-four shows and then were off for six months.

Nervous about the cooking segment of the job and aware she used to send food back to Nate 'N Al's if things weren't just right, as time went on, I watched Del in the kitchen and grew to enjoy creating dishes for her. She tried anything and enjoyed surprises, and she loved fresh vegetables cut up and placed in ice water in the refrigerator. My father would have been proud of me, since he taught me and my brother to cook.

I learned the overview of these parts of life at the studio my first day, but I grew confident with them as the days went on. She loved to come into her apartment between scenes and raid the refrigerator, mostly munching on raw vegetables. Occasionally she longed for See's candy, and we used to keep a box handy. I must admit that when she was in the mood, I never saw anyone go through a box of chocolates as fast as she did. One of the lucky few who could eat and never gain weight, she maintained her svelte, girlish figure of 122 pounds, no matter what. During the day she looked forward to the protein drink Alma fixed for her. After Alma gave me the recipe, I would mix it in the blender in the late afternoon, a combination of protein powder, milk, and fresh fruit. She said it was a great pick-me-up, and she and Rudy, the aging dauxi, would often share it.

While in her apartment during breaks, Doris checked out everything, her careful eyes taking in all her surroundings. She left me a note once saying, "Mare, I think the fridge needs cleaning." The "Del and Mary Kitchen" fed the dogs, too. Her kids never got just plain old dog food. Doris heard from several vets that dogs should have a well-balanced meal. A typical one: fresh ground beef, cottage cheese, grated carrots, oil for their skin, a drop of honey, and, oh, yes, a sprinkle of wheat germ to top it off. These dogs were the easiest to please because they ate everything in sight. Rudy, the dauxi, not only ate what I prepared, but usually took a few nips out of the sofa for dessert.

Often Muffy, the poodle, who was Billy De Wolfe's favorite, would come out for a visit and sit quietly on the set in a director's chair. Denver Pyle, the actor who played Doris's father, gave his stage daughter this beautiful leather chair, with the word DORIS hand-tooled in leather and a daisy dotting the "I." On the back side were engraved the words to her theme song, "Que Sera, Sera." Muffy perched there happy and peaceful. She knew she had to be quiet when the bell rang. Muffy was a "perfect person," according to Doris because she always knew the way to act. That was one of the traits that De Wolfe admired in Muffy, who was the matriarch of the dog family, having raised two black sons, Bobo and Charlie. Charlie had a horrible habit of screeching at any time, and Bobo was used to always being next to Charlie, so the two boys had to stay home.

The regulars at the studio besides Muffy were Bubbles, a lovable black schnoodle; Little Tiger, a sleepy, independent grey poodle, and Rudy, that stubborn, old, couch-chewing dauxi, who was almost deaf. Schatzie, my favorite, a warm-hearted dauxi, and Bucky, number 10, who looked like a red fox with buck teeth, completed the roster. All the dogs were well behaved, and we had fun taking walks on the lot near Doris's apartment. They looked forward to their outing, and so did I. Many times I would walk a couple of them to the offices of Arwin on the lot in another building. The other secretaries had their offices there on the second floor. I made visits daily with mail to be sent out and to pick up letters and bills, too.

One of the accounting secretaries, Betty, told me about her first day on the job, when she met Doris and the dogs. As a child she was very frightened by a large dog and never got over that incident. On her second day at Arwin, she sat in the powder room in a stall when she heard a slight commotion. She realized someone was in the bathroom in another stall. All of a sudden a couple of dogs started to crawl under the divider. Betty made a mad leap up on to the seat, terrified. She heard the other party call out, "Who's there?" Betty did not answer. The other party said, "I'm Mrs. Melcher. Who are you?" Not taking the time to say anything, Betty ran out of the john and dashed back to her desk. She admitted she didn't think Doris ever knew she was the other occupant. But as I brought the dogs over to see her, she began to look forward to their visits and finally felt relaxed with them, overcoming years of phobia.

Doris's fourth TV season finished for the year in December, 1971, with a big Christmas dinner on the set for the cast and crew. With the show on hiatus, its star returned home for six months rest. Since I was her first private secretary, I don't think Doris knew what to do with me now that she wasn't working. The other secretaries stayed on at the studio doing post-production work, but Doris and I developed a system of sorts for the new circumstances. Some days I worked at the studio from an office, and the rest of the time I went to Doris's and worked there. Mornings I prepared to go to either location, but most often Doris would call me to come to her home first and then stay the whole day. Sometimes I felt like a yo-yo, but I enjoyed my up-and-down adventures.

Doris often talked lovingly about her wonderful housekeeper of twenty years, Katie Mattox. "If it wasn't for dear, sweet Katie, I don't know what would have become of Terry." Katie was a happy, good-thinking black lady who tried to keep the family happy and together. Doris said, "She called me, 'The Mrs.'" Doris found refuge in Katie's room when life got complicated. This immaculate housekeeper would often sing her favorite gospel songs as she worked about the house. Doris had told us how much Katie thought of Terry. "That boy really loves her. He'd do anything for Katie," she said. Marty was strict with Terry, insisting he take his lunch to school, and many times Terry would dash out the door and forget the lunch box. But Katie put it in the middle of the door so he would have to trip over it as he ran out the door. Proudly Doris said, "That boy never missed a meal."

During the past year Doris had added Gertie to the household. She was a pleasant, thin black lady, who was working out fairly well. She got along with the dogs, which was all important to Doris. Besides Katie and Gertie, the housework was further divided among Doris, her mom, and Alma's friend Ruth. They all pitched in to do all the many chores in this home where so many dogs complicated housekeeping. In the recent past Doris had done extensive remodeling in her kitchen, living room, and dining room. By the time I arrived, all the work was done, and everything looked bright and cheerful.

About this time Mary and I found a tiny gray poodle loose on the 500 block of Crescent Drive, lost and running in traffic. I was driving and hit the brakes hard to avoid striking it; then Mary and I jumped out. The dog had no ID, and our first thought was to drive up the street with the poodle in the hope that Doris might recognize it. She seemed to know every dog in the area. "I know the names of all the dogs on the street, but very few of the people's names," she boasted.

Before bothering her, we went door to door, but no one answered. Checking the neighborhood, we could see people pulling aside drapery, but no one would come to the door. We took the dog with us to the post office and decided to call Doris from there. Doris answered, telling us she didn't want to answer the bell. She suggested we go even further door-to-door to look for the owner. It seemed like "mission impossible." We used old shoe laces tied together for a leash and knocked on more doors and asked children on the street. No one knew anything about this cute little poodle. We continued our mission for two hours, ranging ever farther afield. Finally, at the last house on the 500 block of Crescent Drive a young boy answered the door.

"Where did you find him?" he exclaimed.

Mary and I couldn't believe that at last we had found the owner. The dog made no effort to go to the boy and seemed to cling harder to Mary. We proceeded to tell him that the dog nearly got hit several times. The boy then invited us in. What a menagerie he had! A Saint Bernard waited in the doorway. A black cat sat in an overstuffed chair. A monkey swung on the rocker, and a shaggy black dog sniffed us. The boy began telling us how stupid the gray dog was. Mary and I, distressed at his attitude, looked at him. Perhaps he was the stupid one.

He then asked, "Do you want him?"

By this time we did, but we hesitated because the owners of our apartment building said "no dogs." We told the boy we would think about it and let him know in the morning. This gray dog seemed made to be our pet—love at first sight. We went back early Sunday morning to claim the poodle and wondered what to call him. Why not ask Doris to think of a name? We drove to her home, and Alma answered the bell. Doris had left for Palm Springs the night before, but she just happened to phone while we were there. She suggested we call him Buffy, so Buffy it was. We gladly picked up our loving little dog.

In a couple of days, Doris called us to bring Buffy over. We arrived and were barely in the door when Buffy sniffed around and promptly walked over to an antique red trunk and lifted his leg. I ran over to him and started apologizing and asked for paper towels. Doris said, "Please don't get so upset. He no doubt smells where my dogs have been. What's a little more?" She was right. Her dogs seemed to have already christened everything. With ten dogs living in her home, you couldn't control everything. Interestingly, there never was a doggy smell.

It didn't take long for our managers to find the third occupant in our apartment. We would have to move. Alma lived in Studio City near the CBS lot, and she thought it best for me to live "over the hill" from my work when we started back at the studio after our six-month halt in production. She became our apartment-hunter and quickly found a satisfactory two-bedroom apartment on the second floor about a mile from her apartment on Moorpark.

At first the managers were not going to let us bring Buffy, but Alma persuaded them to let us have him because she was Doris Day's mother and I was Doris Day's secretary. As soon as the managers saw Buffy, they had no objection and welcomed all three of us. Our first apartment on Olympic Boulevard had been furnished, and so we had no furniture, although we had picked up a few things along the way. Doris gave us a black-and-white plaid sectional sofa that used to be in Marty's office, two Danish chairs, and a yellow leather couch that opened into a double bed.

I was at Doris's home one Sunday night when Gertie, the new housekeeper, came in from her weekend off, distressed over a dog left abandoned next door to friends of hers, telling us that the owners had moved out and left the poor thing tied to the porch, giving the neighbors money to feed him.

"Why didn't you bring him with you?" Doris questioned angrily. Naturally Gertie didn't think of bringing an 11th dog to the house. Doris was so concerned that she made quick phone calls to rescue men through the group Actors and Others for Animals, asking them to pick up the deserted dog as soon as possible. Gertie got on the phone and gave them the exact location and a description of the dog, which she said looked a little like Bubbles. When I heard that, I perked up and told Doris I would be interested in seeing the dog. I dearly loved Bubbles and would give anything to have a pup just like her, in spike of the fact that we had just acquired a dog.

Doris made arrangements for the dog to be checked at the vet, and everything was set for me to take it when released. He was thin, and his teeth showed he had had distemper when young, but he was in perfect condition now. Once he had all of his shots, he became mine. I went to the vet to claim him, sight unseen. When I first saw him, I observed he was a lot bigger than what Gertie had described, and the way he was trimmed, he looked like a bald eagle. When rescued, he had been covered with tar and had to be shaved severely. We brought him home and introduced him to his brother, Buffy. Neither were neutered, and Buffy was about one-fourth his size.

Doris had been patiently waiting to hear about our adoptee. We phoned when we got home, and she asked if we would bring him over. Mary and I drove with the two dogs, but left Buffy in the car. Doris named the new dog "Tiger," and he became "Big Tiger" or "Biggest" eventually. Doris sat on the floor in her living room and played with him as his big saucer eyes danced all over. He loved the attention. A true clown, Tiger bounced around her living room like a gazelle. Doris held his funny face next to hers and held a silent conversation with him. She was in love, but he was mine!

It didn't take long for our managers to discover we had a second dog. I had been taking him to work with me to Doris's home, and he stayed in the den, my office. But our managers were strict; after all, they had to be convinced to accept our first pet. So goodbye dog #2! We had to start looking for a new home for Tiger; moving for us was not an option.

As soon as Doris heard the news, she was not at all happy. I had involved myself in irresponsible animal care, she told me. I should not have taken him in the beginning. Trying to please her in an impossible situation had backfired on me. I should have been honest with her and not offered to take the dog. Finally Doris called me. "Bring him to my house. I guess I'll have to find him a home now." A little offended, I told her I could find him a home myself, but she insisted he was her responsibility. I could tell by her tone that she meant business.

Doris sat in the kitchen waiting for me as I walked in with Tiger. She was at the dog sink, preparing bowls of food for her dogs, and I could sense she was irritated. She never turned around to look at me, but said something about leaving him with her: she would take care of Tiger. I felt helpless. I had wanted to find a home for him, but she had her mind made up that I had blown it, and he became her responsibility. So I said good-bye and left. Later that evening I called to see how Tiger was behaving and to apologize for upsetting her. She told me she was already calling friends about a home for him. We both knew she could not keep 11 dogs. Twice I took Tiger to the "right" home Doris had found; twice he came back. Things didn't work out for one reason or another. Each time I drove off with the dog, Doris hugged him and cried. Finally, she decided enough was enough; she was not going to give him up. No matter what, she would keep him as #11, and we would all just have to work things out. After announcing her decision, she grabbed that dog and cried tears of joy as she held him close.

Not long after that, when I was at the studio in the morning, I received a panicky call from Doris. "Mary Anne, please come here immediately. Gertie is leaving." I wanted to know what was going on. She replied, "Gertie just quit, and I'm worried." I made the drive in record time. Alma had just arrived, and Gertie packed her car with no intention of returning.

Doris called Alma and me aside and said Gertie came into her bedroom early with her breakfast. When she returned to pick up the tray, she gave Doris a story about a sick relative in the Midwest and said she had to leave immediately. Doris asked when she would return. Gertie flat-out said she would not. It all happened suddenly, leaving Doris visibly shaken. Worse yet, she dreaded searching for another housekeeper to care for 11 dogs. "Mission impossible" again.

No one knew Gertie's real reason for leaving. Could it have been the extra dog? Once again in a crisis, Doris wanted to act. She had commented that she could run her house by herself if not working. Maybe Gertie's leaving wasn't so bad after all. Gertie had her flaws: she did not put things back in place when she cleaned. That really irritated Doris. She commented about reading Mary Baker Eddy's life story. Mrs. Eddy was so exacting about everything on her estate outside of Boston. She could seldom get anybody to put things back where they belonged, so she made little notes telling where everything went and what went with what. This was the only way Mrs. Eddy could get things put in their proper place, so Doris said. She went on to tell us, "Mrs. Eddy was so busy running a newspaper and a church that she didn't have time to go around all the time and put things back in place." So it was important that our household, like hers, have the right people.

The search was on for a new housekeeper—again!

7

Terry's Accident

Monday, April 3, 1972, we celebrated Doris's birthday at the Brown Derby in Beverly Hills. I had arranged a surprise party and invited Alma, Mary, Linda, Ruth, and her close studio friends. Doris didn't care much for birthdays. She always said hers was "just another day." However, it was a big day for us. We celebrated with the lady we admired so much, and we could now consider ourselves in her friendship circle.

The following Saturday, April 8th, Doris called us to join her for breakfast at Nate 'N Al's. Over time, the four of us became regulars on Saturday mornings. Even though Doris was old enough to be my mother, age never made a difference.

She was like a big sister to us. As much as she wanted to be close to her only child Terry, she could not be. I only saw him a couple of times until April of 1972. The events that followed Marty's death had propelled Terry on a course straight for rock-bottom, intensifying an already strained relationship with his mother. Terry turned to drugs, worsening through the Manson murders and the added responsibilities of assuming Marty's place.

Doris rarely talked about Terry during this time, but she was nearly in tears telling how after one Thanksgiving a couple of years before, he had invited her to his Cielo Drive home for dinner. She said she barely had a visit with him because he was high on drugs. This hurt her deeply, and she didn't know how to handle it. She wanted desperately to be a strong mother figure, a position she had given up years before to her mom and to Katie, the devoted housekeeper.

During this breakfast conversation, Doris related another frightful incident that happened the night before. She was still shaken by it. She had been awakened in the middle of the night by a dog skirmish on top of her in bed. In the dark she could not tell who was fighting and tried to get out from under the pileup. In doing so, she was bitten several times. The bed was a bloody mess, and she finally got the dogs separated and wrapped her bleeding hand in a towel. As soon as she calmed down, she went into the front bedroom where her mother slept and asked her to take some of the dogs in with her for the rest of the night. She wanted to keep her door closed.

Apparently the two dachshunds, who liked to be close to their mistress, were sleeping in her bed. She thought #11, now known as Biggest, decided at that moment to be part of the family, too. He may have jumped onto her bed to get close to his new mom, but that's when all hell broke loose. This was not the first, nor the last, time these three dogs caused Doris anguish. They bit her several times. But as a good mother, Doris loved her kids regardless. Of course Doris did not want a repeat performance of the experience. The only solution was to muzzle Biggest. She asked me to buy a suitable muzzle and bring it over later that same afternoon.

I stopped at the pet store and found one of the devices that had been designed for a dog his size and took it to Doris. She sat alone in the living room while her new housekeeper of two weeks, Venice, prepared dinner in the kitchen. Doris invited me to have a drink. After that, she intended to put the muzzle on Biggest. She fixed a Dewar's Scotch and water, and we walked around her back yard, admiring the red geraniums and daisies lining the wooden privacy fence. Her domain was very private, like a mini-park, with everything kept perfectly groomed and dogs picturesquely romping around. Doris seemed to want to stall putting the detested item on Biggest, but finally the time came. I had it in my hand; and after we cornered him, she gently put it over his head and adjusted it, like a brace. I didn't like the idea, but I wasn't the one who had to worry about being bitten. He didn't seem happy with the muzzle and tried to pull away as we fastened it.

Looking awkward, he soon began to run with the others. Everything seemed fine. We sat down on the patio and watched. It didn't seem to hinder Biggest's play time, and we soon forgot to patrol the playground. All of a sudden we saw one big ball of fur whirling about with whining and loud barking. Doris and I jumped up, put down our glasses, and raced to the scene of the crime. We discovered Biggest at the bottom of the melee unable to defend himself. Each grabbing a couple of the dogs, we pulled them off one another. Biggest and the two dauxis wanted to continue the fight begun the night before. Doris was beside herself. First order of business: remove that dreadful muzzle. Biggest shook, so we brought him into the kitchen to calm him, and ourselves, down.

Venice announced dinner was ready, and Doris insisted I stay to help her figure out what to do. We took Biggest in the living room and waited for Venice to bring in our trays, relaxing as we looked out at the beautiful yard and pool. Things had calmed down, and we decided to move into the cozy area, an extended part of her living room with the fireplace and TV. We had a drink before dinner to relax. Doris wanted to watch her friend and fellow animal activist, Richard Basehart, in "The Andersonville Trial."

Halfway through dinner, the phone rang. Normally, Doris would not want to be disturbed during a meal and would ask me to get the phone, but this time, she answered. I didn't pay attention until I heard her sobbing, saying, "Oh, my God! Oh, my God! My son! My son! Is he all right? Oh my God! My son!"

Dead silence followed as she listened. The dogs outside sensed something and began howling. She continued sobbing. I ran into the kitchen to tell Venice something had happened to Terry, then dashed back into the living room and sat next to Doris on the sofa. Dissolved in tears, she continued listening intently. She held her head, sitting at one end of her bright yellow sectional sofa. I put my arm around her shoulders to try to comfort her. Limp and wringing wet, she listened to details. She put the phone down and broke down hysterically.

Doris finally jumped up and started pacing, leaving her half-eaten dinner. Her eyes had a glassy stare, her mind a million miles away. She began to relate the account of the accident told by Don Genson of "The Doris Day Show." He had become close to Terry after Marty died. Terry had been thrown 75 feet into the air in a horrendous motorcycle accident. Don received the call from friends who were with him. We didn't know why these friends didn't call Doris first unless they did not have her private number. The accident happened near Terry's home in Idyllwild, near Palm Springs, but he was now at Hemet Valley Hospital. Details were sketchy. Don was leaving immediately and advised Doris not to come until tomorrow morning. He would call as soon as he had arrived and talked to Terry's doctors, then tell her something.

Doris believed her son had sold his motorcycle so she was especially upset to learn that he still had the thing and had flipped it. His condition was critical, and we found out months later that at first the doctors were not sure he would survive. If he did, they thought he might have had to have his legs amputated. As if Doris did not have enough to worry about with her son in the hospital nearly three hours away, she also was afraid of another of these stupid dog fights.

But worst of all, she now had to tell her mother. We decided not to do so until the next morning. Theoretically I was staying overnight to keep the dogs separated, sleeping in the front bedroom with four of the brood. Fortunately, Alma believed the story. She had just moved into her apartment across from ours in Sherman Oaks, and Doris had been pleased that we could look in on her. Since I was spending a lot of time with Doris, either at the studio or at her home, Mary spent time with Alma, which worked out well for both.

Doris and I didn't sleep much because the lights on the phone kept flashing. Don and the doctors constantly called, giving her updates. Terry was alive, in intensive care and heavily sedated. Doris phoned her mother early in the morning and broke the news to her gently.

As soon as Alma arrived, Doris and I headed for Hemet in her Imperial. She was extremely nervous, and I think she took a Valium to try to calm down, but she could not, fearful about what she was about to face. During the one-hundred-mile drive, which seemed endless, we never stopped talking, mostly about religion. I told Doris how my accident turned around my life. Doris always told me, "God sometimes allows things to happen to make you stronger," but when it's your own son in such critical condition, those seem mere words.

I tried to encourage Doris to have faith. We kept talking and repeatedly telling one another that God is good, and He would take care of Terry. We repeated the words of Mary Baker Eddy and Joel Goldsmith—All *is* well. We believed it, and we continued to bolster one another on the long trip. Doris broke down several times, and I encouraged her to believe that his accident would prove to be a turning point in Terry's life. I knew a little of his drug problem at that point. Don's directions proved perfect, and we arrived in hot Hemet Valley and drove straight to the hospital. As we parked the car, we saw Don with some people in the parking lot, those friends who were with Terry when the accident happened, and they gave Doris all the details.

Doris and I rushed in the door to the two volunteer ladies at the reception desk, who immediately recognized her. "Hello, Mrs. Martin. We hope your son is doing well." "Doris Martin" was the name she used on her series. She dashed to the intensive care area, with me right behind her with Don. Stopping before entering, she took a deep breath, wiped her tears away, and went in. It seemed like hours until she finally emerged holding her head and crying, not caring who might see her, at first unable to talk about it. She sobbed as Don and I took her outside. She told me that Terry, suffering severe pain, had been heavily sedated. He was bruised with multiple breaks in both legs. She couldn't go back for another two hours, and then only for five-minute intervals. So we walked to the parking lot and sat on the curb so she could cry in peace and figure out the future. People stared at us. Hemet was a laid-back town, rural and not very sophisticated, a far cry from the glamour of Beverly Hills. Word was getting around that Doris Day's son lay in the hospital and that she was visiting him.

Doris saw Terry in intensive care four times that day. The doctors assured her they were doing everything humanly possible. With the early prognosis far from encouraging, this mother insisted that some way, somehow, her son would make it. The first few days were the most critical, and doctors recommended a lot of prayer, which we undertook. Doris looked so pathetic, so worried, so drawn, tired, and helpless. Tears filled her eyes every time she came from Terry's bedside, but she continued to have faith, even though it looked as though he was in danger of dying.

A year later Dr. Leiberman, the surgeon, admitted to Doris, "I really didn't think Terry was going to make it when I first saw him. After the initial few days, I thought amputation was the next step, but somehow, things worked out. God helped me make the right decision." The right decision was to let the bones settle in place by themselves without a cast, so nature could do its work. This confined Terry to a bed for a minimum of six months.

Dr. Lieberman explained that "timing is the most important thing in Terry's case. We just can't set the bones and put a cast on him. It is not that easy." Both legs were broken in countless places from the 75-foot fall; it would be weeks before doctors could think about setting them, if then.

When it began getting dark, Doris decided we must drive back home.

She would make arrangements to return as soon as possible that week. In spite of the fact that she wanted to be near Terry, she had to be back to CBS on Monday morning to film her series. The drive home was very quiet, and it was late when we returned to Crescent Drive. Alma, in tears, anxiously waited to hear about her beloved "Tershy," as she called him. Doris had been in touch a couple of times by phone, but now she filled in the details. She kept in constant touch with the kind doctors at the hospital, and Don promised to remain in Hemet indefinitely.

Doris made arrangements at the studio, changing her schedule around, and returned to Hemet the following day with Barbie Lampson to stay a week. She asked me to move into her home to keep things on an even keel there. When Doris called with updates on Terry's progress, she told us he was gradually pulling out of the critical stage, but had a long siege ahead. She was eager to have him home, but no dates were mentioned for his release.

After that week Doris made frequent trips to Hemet, and often I went with her. The second time I went, taking two dogs, Biggest and Little Tiger, we found room for our group at the Romona Motel, one block from the hospital. The managers went out of their way to make sure no one bothered us in our adjoining rooms. The motel, a modest hostelry, was the best Hemet could offer. Some patrons seemed to be using the motel for one-night stands, judging from the noise and activity. However, it was the only decent motel in this dusty little town.

While Doris visited with Terry, I remained in the hospital courtyard playing with the dogs. Biggest loved to chase a tennis ball and gum it, while Tiger wanted to find a spot in the shade and rest. We were quite a novelty in Hemet, and locals knew that if they saw the dogs, Doris was near. People wanted to ask me questions, and a few got up the courage. They would ask, "Are you her daughter?" "Her sister?" "Her roommate?" Finally, word got around that I was her secretary, and then they started asking me all kinds of questions. They were just down-home folks; we were, too. When Doris and I took walks around the motel with the dogs, we began to learn where other dogs lived in the neighborhood. Doris would talk to the owners and tell them what darling "kids" their four-legged friends were. She would always remind them to take good care of them. I got a kick out of watching people's reactions when they recognized her. Hemet is hardly the place one would expect to see one of the most beloved actresses in the world.

After visiting with Terry in the day, Doris and I would go to a little restaurant for dinner and come back to the motel. One night she flipped on the TV to watch the news and invited me to watch with her. A single door divided our rooms, allowing the dogs to run from one room to another. She flipped from station to station, and as she clicked past one, I said, "Stop! That's the back of your head from *Please Don't Eat the Daisies.*" "Oh, Marzy, you're nuts," she said. I told her I knew the back of her head with that French roll and to please go back. She did and seemed totally surprised. There she was, appearing with David Niven in the Jean Kerr movie. After all, I was the Doris Day fan, and I knew her, even from behind.

Doris made many sacrifices for these frequent trips. But the mother and son became closer than they had ever been. She had not been pleased with his lifestyle prior to the accident, but being in the hospital for nearly six months cured him of the addictive lifestyle. During one of her trips, I stayed at her home, and she went with Barbie. Venice the housekeeper was not turning out as well as we had hoped. Alma asked her to fix a roast because Doris would be hungry when she came in and would be eager for a home-cooked meal. To everyone's surprise, Venice said, "Fix it yourself."

Later, Alma left to do some shopping, and I took a shower. I asked Venice to answer the phones and door, but she gave me a snotty answer, "You should have taken your shower while Mrs. Day was here. I'm too busy to answer phones and doors." This was not going to work. When Doris called before leaving Hemet, I clued her in on Venice's actions. Doris replied, "Fire her, Mary Anne." What? I had never fired anyone before in my life. I went into the den and practiced for about an hour. Finally, I got up the courage to give her the word. As she left, she mumbled, "Miss Day sure has a lot of worries around here." Once again, Doris was without help, and the search needed to begin anew.

Doris went to Hemet weekly. Her fifth TV season had begun in June, but week-day filming did not stop her from traveling to see Terry. We left each Friday after rehearsal in mid-afternoon to beat the rush hour, trying to get to the Romona Motel by seven. Terry gradually felt better, but still had a long time ahead, flat on his back. Still with no casts, he did exactly what Leiberman said, not sure of the outcome. During the summer heat, Doris tried to talk Billy De Wolfe into joining her on the trip. Billy liked Terry very much, and the feeling was mutual. Billy agreed, but at the last minute he had to cancel. In a way, Doris was glad he didn't go. As she said later,

"Uncle Billy would never have appreciated what we got into on that weekend." I recalled that Doris and I would usually walk Biggest and Little Tiger through a medical building across the street from our motel on our way to the hospital. On this particular day it was about 106 and very dry. As we walked through the arcade, Doris noticed limp flowers and shrubs, barely alive, in desperate need of watering. She spotted the water outlets and began planning a strategy for after our visit. We both believed no gardener would come on the weekend. We had to save the posies.

We came back after about two hours, and the area was still dry as a bone. Taking off our shoes and socks, we rolled up our slacks, fastened the dogs to a post in the center, and proceeded to go to work. We turned on the garden faucets and found an old tin container to use on the flowers in the center of the walkway, where there were no faucets. We executed a bucket brigade to service the center aisle. No one bothered us, and with everything soaked, we started to shut off all the faucets, eight all together. That's when the trouble began. The more we turned the handles, the more water flowed. The gardens filled with water, becoming a swamp. We tried like the devil to shut them off, but got nowhere. Doris gave it one more try and bent over to reach a handle, giving it a good jerk. The handle broke off in her hand. Water went shooting into the air through an opening in the roof, like a spray from an out-of-control firemen's hose.

We walked around in inches of water when a girl came through with a stack of papers from one of the offices. She took one look and then calmly asked, "Are you Doris Day?" After Doris answered in the affirmative, the girl disappeared. I thought she would call the police. Since they didn't come, Doris ran to the emergency lobby of the hospital and called Terry's room. She knew that his friend Eddie was visiting with him and begged Eddie to come across to the medical plaza as fast as he could. Shocked to see what a mess we had made, as the water continued to rise up the courtyard walls, Eddie searched for the faucet. He had to find the handle to cap the thing. He solved our dilemma in seconds, but sternly made us promise never to fool with the water again.

Doris and I learned a lesson, yet couldn't keep ourselves from laughing at our little garden escapade. If Billy had come, he surely would have disowned us. Terry, too, laughed when he heard the story. His spirits had begun to perk up, and he looked forward to his mom's arrival each weekend, even worrying when she came late. Doris took her script with her, and we often read lines together around the pool and in between visits. A devoted mother, she wasn't going to let distance or a hectic TV schedule keep her away. It was hard on her, but she didn't let anyone know it, especially Terry. Her career had kept her from spending time with him during the early years, while her mother devoted herself to raising Terry, first in Cincinnati and later in Hollywood. And then Marty insisted on sending him to boarding school. Now she had a chance to truly get to know him, and he to know her.

I remembered a particular conversation with Doris about Terry's growing-up years. We were cleaning the closet Doris referred to as "the tunnel," an area where the sauna was later located. She would frequently go to an old jewelry box and pull out some of the contents. I think she had every one of Terry's report cards there, and she'd gaze at them, no doubt recalling happy memories. Also in the box were letters from Terry when Marty sent him away to Principia Upper School in St. Louis. Doris commented, "I'll never understand why Marty kept wanting to get Terry out of the house all the time and send him away to school. Why on earth would a California boy want to board in a school back east when all his pals and family were here in California?" After hearing this story, my only thought was, "You were his mother and you didn't have any say in his life and upbringing?" But I never dared question her on the forbidden subject of her relationship with Marty.

Through these visits to Hemet, I saw a beautiful and rare relationship developing, and Doris felt it, too, and said she was grateful to God for Terry's progress. I sent Terry cards to cheer him, and I could certainly sympathize with him, remembering my own stay in Long Beach Community Hospital a couple years before. I didn't want to take up her time with Terry, but I wanted to see him, too, and was pleased when she said, "Mary Anne, why don't you come in and see my son?"

Late that summer the hospital released Terry after six long months. He returned to Beverly Hills and chose to recuperate with friends for the first few months. Terry felt it would be best for him not to stay at his mom's because of the dogs. Once he was stable on his feet, he moved home. Doris was eager to have him and had her guest house ready to welcome him with fresh flowers. It was his abode for the next several months.

Bubbles kisses Doris on the CBS lot. Shadows are me taking Doris's picture.

8

Moving in with Doris Day

Doris completed her fifth and final season of "The Doris Day Show" in December, 1972. This last year proved more rugged than the others. She had to spend a lot of time with lawyers, planning strategy to see if any of her fortune could be recovered in court from the Melchers' former financial consultant, Jerome Rosenthal, who along with Marty, had made questionable deals with her money. Along with legal worries, she had continuing concern for Terry. He had come a long way and seemed happy to be living in the guesthouse. Terry was able to get around well using a cane, and Doris loved seeing him improve, but he wasn't home free yet.

I asked Doris about my taking time off to fly to Indianapolis to spend Christmas holidays with my mother, and she agreed. This would be the second Christmas following my father's death, and my mother anxiously awaited my return. I made my flight reservations in advance to get the best price. Doris's mom was also going to be away in Houston to spend the holidays with Shirley and her family

A few months before, through an employment agency, Doris had found a housekeeper: a single, attractive woman about 25 named Nada, originally from Yugoslavia. Nada spoke decent English and was good with dogs. She had a neat appearance and seemed to be working out well, and Doris and her mom liked her.

Two weeks before Christmas, Nada received a letter from her family in

Yugoslavia, telling of her mother's poor health. She asked Doris if she could fly home for a month to be with her family and ailing mother. Doris was not prepared for everyone to desert her for the holidays, and she wanted someone to stay and help her with the dogs.

The situation was too much for her to manage for an extended time. It was all right for Alma and me to go, as long as Nada would be there, but with all three of us away, Doris could not cope with the responsibilities alone. One of us had to stay. Doris wanted her mother to go to Houston, and Nada was going regardless of who stayed. Although she was not asking me to give up my holiday, I could see her strained state of mind.

I said, "Clara, I don't want you to worry. I'll stay with you." Doris knew what a sacrifice that was because I looked forward to spending time with my mother, who as a new widow needed me, especially at the holidays. Oddly enough, to Doris holidays were just like any other time and not the family gatherings most people enjoyed; still, she needed help and company.

The call to Mom would break her heart, but I had no solution. I told her that as soon as Nada returned, I would come. I offered to fly for a weekend prior to everyone's leaving town, but she told me not to spend all that money on a plane ticket for just two days. She was right, but it didn't change the fact that she would be alone for the holidays.

Doris didn't want her mother to know Nada was leaving and told the housekeeper not to say anything. She knew her mother would cancel the trip to Houston, and Doris wanted her to go. Nada and I kept quiet about the plans, and Alma got off to Houston on Sunday morning, December 17th. That afternoon, Nada left.

Over the weekend I got my things together to move to Crescent Drive for the Christmas season. I arrived with my clothes late that Sunday afternoon, and Doris welcomed me with open arms and a sigh of relief. Once I settled in the front bedroom just across from her master bedroom, we fed the dogs and then sat in the living room. The dogs were comfortable and quiet, and we just talked.

As I mentioned, "Clara" became the name several of us affectionately called her. Billy De Wolfe had dubbed her "Clara Bixby" years before, and the name stuck. She used to call me "Mare" or "Marzy Doats" after the song of the mid-1940s. Many times at night I heard her sing "Marzy Doats" or call out, "Night, Mare," from her bedroom.

As days went on, I became the cook, housekeeper, dog-sitter, nurse to all, and, last but not least, personal secretary. With no official maid anymore, Doris and I pitched in to do all the work. She often called herself "Nora Neat" or "Crazy Clean." Wanting everything in perfect order, she rushed about cleaning, sweeping, and dusting. I had no choice but to fall in line. There is an awful lot of washing, cleaning, and feeding going on with a home full of 11 lively canines romping through it. They tracked in dirt and stirred up dust, slopped food around, and (only rarely) made potty mistakes. Housework in the Day home never ended.

Doris wanted everything just so. So it was impossible to keep her home the way she would like it. The dark hardwood floors in the dining room, foyer, and den constantly showed fuzz from her golden carpets, and there were stains around the legs of the furniture. A daily mop-up job. Two oriental rugs, one in the foyer and a runner in the dining room, had to be scrubbed by hand with a brush to remove all the dog hair. Someone had to comb the rugs, and occasionally I would catch Doris on her hands and knees scrubbing. I'd grab the brush from her and finish the job myself. The Mexican tile floor in the kitchen magnified the balls of dog hair and wet spots. The laundry, too, collected dust and spots. We worked hard to keep things clean, but you could never keep ahead. I must say that Doris never asked me to do anything she herself would not do.

Secretarial work, such as dictation and typing, was a "dead art" most of the time, with Doris and me simply keeping too busy cleaning the house to tackle the office work. I didn't mind doing it because it helped her, and I was happy to just be there. A typical day began with a bike ride for the five blocks to Nate 'N Al's for breakfast. Doris enjoyed eating there, seeing old friends and relaxing. She knew most of the regulars and all of the waitresses. Helen, Kaye, and Dena, three of her favorites, always made us feel at home. Once finished, we headed back to work at her home.

One Sunday Doris and I met Mary and Linda at Nate's for breakfast, and Mary came back to the house. Doris went to her room and let the dogs out. I put "my group" out on the side yard by the garage. Mary sat in the living room and looked a little surprised when I appeared with a mop and dust cloth. She exclaimed, "You have to come back and work on Sunday? You never did this at home." I told her it didn't make any difference what day it was at the Day household because *every day* we cleaned with Sunday no exception.

Often Doris would comment about how she would ideally like to have her home look, especially the bedroom. She would decorate it with elegant draperies and a lace bedspread. But with 44 feet parading around, sometimes fighting tooth and claw, a beautiful boudoir was a distant dream. She could see it would be foolish to invest in such frills. She spoke fondly about her home in Toluca Lake in the "old days" when she lived with Marty and Terry and her two standard poodles, Smudgie and Beanine. Life must have been a lot easier and less complicated. Now she was alone with tremendous responsibility on her shoulders, including 11 canines.

Doris loved to move furniture, and often during the middle of the night she would rearrange chairs and settees, almost as if the furniture bored her. I'd be asleep in the bedroom at midnight, but Doris would be up making changes. It was so strange for me to wake up and find the living room altered. Many times I ended up helping. I remember the time Doris wanted to move the baby grand piano about three inches from the doorway. She had new carpeting, and the movers had put the piano back a little out in the aisle between the living and dining rooms. This bothered Doris. We removed the old Tiffany lamp from the piano, and she pushed and I pulled. It barely moved. It weighed a ton. We tried again, and the back end of the piano crashed to the floor. The house shook like a level-6 earthquake had hit it, leaving us staring, stunned, at a lopsided piano. The front leg had broken off, and we knew we couldn't leave it like this for long or the back legs would give way. I ran out to the garage and brought back three old bar stools. Doris and I sweated blood to lift the fallen end to rest on them. She then asked me to call her insurance agent. He paused after hearing about our mishap and then laughed, saying, "Break another leg, you have a two-leg deductible."

With Alma and Nada away on their trips, Doris informed me she was considering having a face-lift. I looked at her. She didn't need to have that beautiful face lifted at all! But she had spoken to a mutual friend of ours, Grace Emerson, who had undergone cosmetic surgery, and Doris was impressed with the results and Grace's fast recovery. Apparently she had been thinking about this for some time and finally made an appointment with the friend's doctor, Steven Zax. I guess she figured it was safe to have it done with her mom and housekeeper out of town. No one would know anything. For the life of me I couldn't figure why at this particular moment she wanted cosmetic surgery. Her TV show had finished its run, and she had no plans for working again. Maybe it was just a Hollywood thing that actresses did as they aged.

The day for the appointment came, and I drove Doris to Dr. Zax's Wilshire Boulevard office. Within an hour she called me to pick her up. She was laughing when she got into the car. She thought she was going to have the job done that day, and so did I, but it turned out to be just a consultation. As we thought about it, we chuckled—thinking that she could dash in and have her face done, and pop out again, just like that.

During the seven-minute drive home, Doris jolted me with startling news. "Mary Anne, I'm not going to have my face-lift done right away. I'm having my breasts done first." I nearly drove off the road. Why now? Her figure was stunning, admired by all who saw her. I know that I looked surprised, and then she began explaining that Dr. Zax said it was a simple operation. She apparently told him that her clothes did not fit the way they used to. He explained to her that there was no reason why she couldn't look the same as she had at age 35. I wondered why the doctor would encourage another operation when she just went in for one. Perhaps the usual answer: it's a Hollywood thing actresses do to keep up appearances and for which doctors collect large fees.

Though it was probably none of my business, I felt compelled to say I thought she was playing with fire, especially because of a cancer scare she experienced in the early 1950s. But her mind was made up, and nothing, no one, would alter it. The breast lift was set for December 29. She had all of the instructions from Dr. Zax, and we went over them, because I was going to put on my nurse's hat; she was to be in my care and mine alone when she returned home. She asked me to shop for a special kind of sleep bra because the doctor told her it was important that she wear one at all times to keep her muscles in shape. After making several calls to department stores, I located the one the nurses suggested and ordered a half dozen. Now, ready for the big day, we had first to celebrate Christmas, even in the muted way Doris decreed.

Christmas Eve showed the most holiday spirit I ever saw at Doris's home. Terry asked two of his friends over for dinner: Beach Boy Bruce Johnston and Paul Hampton, a handsome young actor Doris had met after his co-starring role in *Lady Sings the Blues*. Doris asked me to fix the favorite lemon chicken like her mom made for the dinner. It was served on blue-and-white Spode china. We were having a nice time visiting and enjoying the meal in the dimly lit dining room when the power failed. So we used candles, which lit up in the darkened halls like tiny matches with glimmers of flame, dancing in reflection on the windows. The party broke up early. The boys had to leave their cars parked in the driveway overnight because the electric gates froze shut from the power failure. They exited through the alley in Terry's car.

Christmas day came like any other. As much as I enjoyed being with Doris, especially on a day like Christmas, I wished I had been with my mother, alone in Indianapolis. However, here we had many Christmas presents stacked up in the cozy area near the fireplace to be opened over the next couple of days. That might be something to look forward to. Doris explained the reason for her not enjoying the holiday season went back to her band days. "The holidays were always the busiest, most hectic times for the big bands. We were usually out in Podunk, somewhere. My little boy Terry and my mother lived in Cincinnati. They would always have Christmas with the rest of the family there. A few weeks later they would join me, if I was working at a hotel somewhere. We would have our own Christmas, a little late, but beautiful. Of course, I did spend Christmas with the boys in the band, which was always fun. They were such terrific guys." Still, I knew it could not have been all that meaningful and festive.

We were invited to Carmen Sawtelle's home for a pitch-in brunch around 1:00 PM. Doris had met Carmen a few years before. The lady was very much into "metaphysics" and was Doris's and my "Joel Goldsmith" practitioner. I was never sure if Carmen was a Christian Scientist or something else. A lovely woman in her mid 80s, she had spent much of her life in Hawaii and had been in Los Angeles for the past 20 years. Carmen had quite a following of people who met on a regular basis, all searching for "truth and peace" through metaphysics. Her mentor, Joel Goldsmith, was a spiritual leader and ex-Christian Science practitioner Doris listened to on tape. Doris and Carmen shared many conversations about his teachings. I was surprised that Doris agreed to go to Carmen's because she really did not like crowds, especially people she did not know. But it was Christmas, and she said we would go, but not stay too long. She could always use the dogs as an excuse to return home.

We had a wonderful time. Doris looked stunning in a long red paisley dress. All the guests watched her every move. Carmen gave a little talk to the 20 or so people who gathered for a traditional turkey dinner with all of the trimmings. Guests brought desserts. Doris seemed very relaxed and enjoyed herself. We stayed about two hours.

Once home, we headed to the cozy area, filled with gifts from adoring fans from around the world, most still unopened. It became a chore for her to open so many; she asked me to go through and make a list of people to thank. The biggest touch of Christmas was the spicy aroma from the huge della robia wreath she had received this year and every year from Amanda Blake (Kitty on "Gunsmoke") and her husband. Without a tree, this was the closest thing to Christmas decorating I saw in her home.

Doris and I had our gift exchange. She gave me a Snoopy card with the note: "Dear One, What can I say but thank you for being my true friend!!! Buy yourself something 'pretty' and remember, Mare—the best is yet to come!!!! Love, Clara." Inside was a check for $100, and I bought a pretty green velvet pant suit with it. Doris knew I had been looking at it and liked it. I gave her a sterling silver watering can from Geary's North, a specialty shop in Beverly Hills that Doris frequented. The inscription was "To Clara, the Lady of the House with love always, M.A." I was so happy to see her expression when she opened it.

December 29th arrived, and Doris seemed apprehensive about her upcoming operation, and so was I. Before leaving in the limousine, she told me that she or the nurse would call just before she was returning so that I could have the dogs placed in different rooms. I assured her I would see that everything was perfect. She should not worry about the house or her babes. A little after 8:00 AM the chauffeured limousine pulled through her gates. Doris wore a loose-fitting kaftan and comfortable slippers. She gave me last-minute instructions and kissed me good-bye, then got into the darkened car and rode off. The day seemed endless as I waited for the call that she was all right. I fed the dogs early and took care of things she wanted done. Her room stood ready with clean linens and plenty of air spray. About 4:00 PM the phone rang, and a nurse said Doris was about to leave the doctor's office. I had the gates opened and waited at the door.

The car stopped in front, and a nurse got out on the driver's side, then came around and opened the back door to help a groggy Doris out. I grabbed her on the other side and led her to her bedroom. She got in bed and dropped off to sleep instantly, still wearing her kaftan. The nurse took her vitals and had a list of instructions for me for the post-operative care. Doris was to sleep most of the night, and I was to watch that she did not get chilled. I was to feel each breast about every hour to see if it felt unnatural, lumpy, or hardened. My face must have turned beet red when she told me that. I immediately said, "I can just see Doris waking up or me awakening her standing over her and feeling her breasts." The nurse did not pay attention to my prissy Catholic education concerns and emphasized that it was an important procedure, vital for this kind of surgery. I sighed and told her I would watch and report if anything seemed unusual. She gave more instructions and then left me to continue my all-night vigil. I fed the dogs and bedded them down in various rooms. They could sense something was going on and behaved like little angels that night. I didn't let any of them in her bedroom because she didn't need that kind of distraction. Besides, I had pills for pain that had to be given on a certain schedule. I was her private duty nurse for the evening.

I spent much of my night on the comfy couch in her bedroom a couple of feet from her. I did not sleep, keeping at least one eye on my patient. Part of the night I spent standing guard between her bed and the white wicker desk. She was definitely out, and I watched and waited for any move or change or sound. The only move she made was with her hands now and then. I couldn't get up the nerve to "feel" her and take the chance of her waking up as I followed doctor's orders. Doris was an extremely private person. Always a lady, she never went around undressed, at least with anyone around. I never walked into her dressing room without calling out, "Clara, are you dressed?" Her reply was usually, "Sure, Marzy, come in."

The night seemed endless. I paced from the couch to her bedside all night long. I prayed. Boy, did I pray. I had complete trust in God and in Dr. Zax that everything would turn out well because I could not bring myself to feel her. I looked forward to the morning when Dr. Zax would stop on the way to his office to check her. By daybreak I was exhausted. As the sun started coming up, Doris moved in her bed and finally woke up. Groggy from the sedation, she started asking me how long she slept. She had the normal pain from the incision, and I had pills to give her if her discomfort got severe, but she did not need them.

Doris decided not to tell anyone about her "uplift," and the story, if anyone asked, was that she had a mole removed. This didn't hold for long. People began to notice. They commented, "Doris doesn't look the way she used to. She used to be a little on the flat side compared to the silhouette now. What happened?" The public and her friends were not blind, especially since this new look happened overnight. Doris would answer that her hormone pills caused a change in her shape. Alma defended her because she knew nothing of the operation. Doris made sure of that.

New Year's Eve was the next night, and I had a date. David Knox, a mutual friend of Doris's and mine, was about 20 years older than I. David had been a fan of Doris since her Hollywood Palladium days in the mid-40s. He had invited me out to dinner that night, and Doris insisted that I go and have a good time, especially since I had been so confined for the past couple of days in my nursing duties. We asked her to join us, but she did not feel up to socializing. She asked if I would come home fairly early, and we agreed. She had put some champagne out at the bar for us. David and I had a nice dinner at the Beverly Wilshire and returned about 10:30 PM. We sat at the bar listening to Guy Lombardo on the radio. Smooth saxophone playing soothed us as the band and crowd moved their way toward "Auld Lang Syne." We sipped champagne and waited for the new year.

I buzzed Doris on the intercom to let her know we were back; we had been announced by the dogs. I asked if she needed anything, and she said she was content and had some of her dogs with her. We had four dogs in with us: Bobo, Charlie, Rudy, and Schatzie. As usual, they were all comfortable, nestled in the lap of luxury.

David and I continued enjoying the music and champagne, and then the buzzer sounded. Doris asked me to come back to her bedroom. I left David at the bar and walked through the hall into her bedroom. We conversed, and after a few minutes I reminded her I still had a guest. I asked if she needed anything or if she would like to join us. She declined and told me to say "Hi" to David and to wish him a Happy New Year. I returned to the living room, and within another few minutes the light and buzzer sounded. I picked up right away. Again, it was something else she wanted this time, and something the next time beyond that, until it seemed like every ten minutes the buzzer sounded. Like a scene from an Abbott and Costello movie, the situation began to be a little embarrassing, and I figured David would think I was giving him some kind of message.

Finally 1973 was ushered in with a thunderous dog fight at the living room windows overlooking Doris's backyard. She apparently had let her group outside, and they came over to the large windows by the living room to inaugurate a confrontation with their pals or adversaries within the room. My group had the two militant dachshunds, Rudy and Schatzie, who seemed to smell out Biggest on the other side. Thank God for the glass barrier! My two ran back and forth, knocking down everything in sight. David grabbed one, and I grabbed the other, and we put them out on the side yard to cool off. Doris finally called out to Biggest. Without the two militant dogs, Biggest was free to prance back and forth and proudly walk back into Doris's bedroom.

The buzzer sounded again, the end of the party for all of us. David got the hint to leave, and, frankly, I was looking forward to some peace and quiet. I gathered my group and took them to my bedroom. With all of us settled in with the kids, Doris could get some sleep. That's how we celebrated New Year's Eve—with a bang! Once again, I heard her husky voice call out, "Night, Mare." To which I replied, "Night, Clara."

For the next few days, Doris complained of soreness; however, when she visited Dr. Zax, he told her she was healing nicely. Doris was relieved to have one operation over with and made plans for the second and final one. After her breast lift, she was not allowed to drive for about six weeks, nor was she able to ride her bike or do any physical movement that involved her arm muscles. Used to a daily swim and a bike ride when she wanted it, Doris now found her schedule was altered, so I drove her wherever she wanted to go.

Many people commented after her operation. A year later Doris, Jackie Susann, and Billy De Wolfe appeared on the "Merv Griffin Show." Doris looked stunning, and her figure was shown off at its best. Following the show, Billy phoned saying, "Clara, all my boob-watching friends called and asked me to tell you that you looked absolutely adorable." She laughed, but seemed embarrassed. Many older fans did not like the new image, and some made bitter comments, which didn't seem to bother her at all. She continued to enjoy showing herself off in more form-fitting, ever-more-daring jersey gowns. Her appearance on "The Johnny Carson Show" in a teal blue, semi-transparent blouse distracted Johnny as he interviewed her for nearly half an hour. The fact she no longer wore a bra was obvious. The alterations to her figure were a small part of the picture. Her sunny personality attracted people more than any physical change.

My mother came out to visit me and is shown on the set of "The Doris Day Show" in the summer of 1972.

Doris smiles and loves her dogs in her TV show living room set.

<u>ACT TWO</u>

FADE IN:

9   INT. DORIS' OFFICE - DAY   9

Doris is on the phone.

> DORIS
> (on phone)
> ...Well, why not have one more
> waiter just to be safe...uh huh...
> good, then we'll see you Saturday
> night.

She hangs up phone. During above Jackie ENTERS.

> JACKIE
> Did you arrange everything with
> the caterers?

> DORIS
> All set.

> JACKIE
> Don't tell me, I know just what
> we're going to eat...carrot and
> raisin salad, chicken a la king,
> green peas, a hard roll and a
> fruit for dessert.

> DORIS
> Not for Sam Johnson -- we're
> having shrimp cocktail, caesar
> salad, filet mignon and Baked
> Alaska.

> JACKIE
> Doris, how can you give Cy a
> bill for a dinner like that?

> DORIS
> Easy...with his eyes, he'll never
> see it.

Doris personally supervised her TV show scripts and sometimes made changes.

*Here comes the bride—
Doris on the set of a TV
fashion show in 1972.*

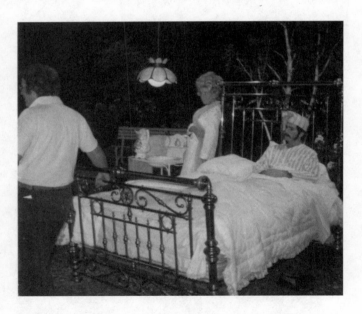

*Doris stands beside a "set bed" at CBS Studios for the CBS TV
fashion show.*

One of Doris's long-time friends was Joy Tierney, the seamstress, shown here with Doris on the set at CBS Studios.

High on a stool and ready to go on at the TV fashion show.

Carmen Sawtelle and Doris chat on the set. Carmen was one of Doris's spiritual mentors.

9

Day by Day with Doris Day

On January 11th Doris prepared for her face-lift. Once again the window-darkened, chauffeured limousine arrived to take her in the morning to the hospital. Late in the afternoon, about 4:30 PM, the phone rang, and it was Doris. She was mumbling, not very coherent, so I was concerned. Then the nurse got on the line to tell me what the patient wanted. Doris worried about my being alone with her because recovery would be much longer this time. She thought I should have help with the dogs so that I could care for her. I was to call Ruth, the friend of her mother's who had been helpful in coming over when needed. She had known Doris and Alma for years. Ruth, however, was working toward being a Worthy Matron in Eastern Star, and those activities took all of her time. This left me in charge of everything again, but this time I was ready for the assignment.

The nurse alerted me that when they would arrive in about half an hour, I needed to have everything set. I had the gates open and waited patiently. Again the nurse helped Doris from the car. Her face was completely bandaged except for her swollen nose and mouth. She was groggy from the medication. I put my arm gently around her waist and, walking right behind her, directed the nurse to her bedroom. I felt like her shadow as we made the walk back. We got the patient into bed without any trouble, because Doris was cooperative and sleepy from the sedation. The nurse gave me another list of instructions, more than before, and more pills to administer. She told me Doris would be delirious because of the medication. If she started to talk strangely, I should not attempt to keep up a conversation, but instead ignore her questions or comments so that she could get some rest. I had pills for pain and antibiotics, and decided to do my own make-shift chart on her as the nurses do in the hospitals. She was my patient now, and I had to do all I could to keep her comfortable.

As soon as the nurse left, I called Ruth to come and help, and it was possible for her to come. Ruth took care of the dogs; I had charge of Doris. I again camped on the sofa in her bedroom, waiting and watching for any movement, with Ruth coming in occasionally to check on us. She reported all quiet on the western front with the canines. Doris would awaken now and then from the pain. She looked so helpless and pitiful. I was reminded of the many accident cases I saw while in the hospital. Fortunately, hers was only a face-lift. As I watched over her, she suddenly called out my name. I grasped her hand and said, "I'm here, Clara." She tried to speak but couldn't.

I held her hand as she tried to speak. Finally in a whisper she said affectionately, "Marzy, I don't really know how to express my thanks to you for taking such good care of me, but I just want you to know that I appreciate it very much." I squeezed her hand to let her know I was right by her side. Tears came to my eyes. Here she was, so helpless and uncomfortable, yet she wanted to thank me. But that was my Clara: to me, the most thoughtful person and never too busy to say "thank you" for the smallest courtesy. I'll always remember her funny little bandaged face and those loving words.

About midnight she asked me to help her to the bathroom. I had to lead her by putting my arms gently around her waist and walking right behind her. She hung onto my arms, trusting me. We got this procedure down pat, and I left her in the bathroom until she called. With this kind of mutual dependency, Doris and I had become very close, and it was often hard for me to picture her as my boss. I felt instead as if she were my big sister, and these two "sisters" got along well, with respect and trust as the foundation of the friendship. Fanhood had faded into the distant past.

The following morning Dr. Zax arrived to check her and remove part of the bandages so that she could hear better. She was still going to be somewhat sedated, but the doctor approved of her progress. There would still be pills to administer, and I kept a chart once again. She slept most of the second day, so I took a cat nap now and then, with one eye always on Doris.

The second night was bizarre. Doris started into a strange dialogue and began asking me all kinds of weird questions. She knew I was there because she kept calling out to me. "Marzy, where are we? Why are they roller skating on my roof?" And then she would doze off. In a few minutes she would start again. I did not pay any attention at first, because the nurse had warned she would be somewhat out of her head.

At one time when she seemed alert and began talking, I answered— just what the doctor said not to do, "Clara, we are right here in your bedroom and no one is roller-skating on your roof. Maybe it's the wind you hear, but there is definitely no one roller skating." The more I tried to explain, the more I realized she didn't comprehend a word. I became concerned and took her temperature. Fortunately, she didn't question what I was doing, and like a good patient, anything I did was OK with her. I had to go into her bathroom to read the thermometer since the one light we had on in her room was dim. To my amazement, she had a 102 fever. I became more worried and buzzed Ruth, relaying the weird conversation. After I told her about Doris's fever, we decided to call Dr. Zax, even though it was very late. He reassured us.

When morning rolled around, Dr. Zax checked her bandages and removed a few in the area around her eyes. By this time Doris felt more like herself, and the doctor was pleased with her progress. He gave me more medication, a salve for around her eyes that I was to apply at indicated intervals.

Doris remained an excellent patient, always so grateful for anything we did. In fact, she made me a promise I will always remember. She told me that when the time came, if I needed her in the hospital or having a baby, that she would be there to care for me as I was doing for her. I held her hand and thanked her. I knew she meant it because she always said, "Marzy, I do things because I want to do them, not because I have to."

On the third day she felt more like herself and was able to get around much more easily. She still had only bathroom privileges and began to get fidgety as the day wore on, like a race horse at the starting gate. It was not her style to be in bed during the daytime. Later in the day I had gone to the kitchen, and when I returned to her bedroom, I heard water running. Was she getting ready to take a bath? The nurse had banned showers. The water splashed away, and soon Doris called me into her bathroom saying, "Come in, and see what I've done." I walked into a little "dyeing" factory she had set up in her dressing room just off the bedroom. She found an old box of RIT dye and experimented with it on some old bras and panties. To her surprise, they turned out very pretty. Looking at her with a big smile I said, "Clara, what do you think you're doing?"

Doris knew darn well what she was supposed to be doing, but she was bored, and dyeing clothes seemed much more fun. She had both her sinks filled with vivid colors and clothes drying on towels all over her golden shag carpeting. Like a little girl having a good playtime coloring clothes, she had me so convinced this was a fascinating pastime that for a moment I was tempted to bring her some of my own clothes to dye. Then I begged her to stop and get back into bed. Exertion was not what the doctor ordered, and it might hinder her progress. She finally agreed to get back into bed, but sent me out to buy more boxes of RIT. She had more clothes she wanted to work with and some new colors in mind.

When I returned home with her order, she asked me to get a particular negligee from her cave closet; she wanted to take the lining out of it. At a certain time in her life she had removed sleeves from her clothes, so I guess now she was going through the "take-out-the-linings" phase. Hardly the Betsy Ross type, all of a sudden she was dyeing clothes and taking out linings. What next? She insisted I get the negligee she wanted from her closet; however, that description fit at least three garments, so I brought them to choose from.

She picked one, and I put the others back. Suddenly I heard a loud RIP and ran back to her. Doris looked quite pleased until she looked closely and found no lining in the pretty gown, which was now almost in shreds. I didn't know whether to laugh or cry. We both stared at one another and broke into laughter. Certain she must have a fever, I decreed "playtime" was now over. She needed her rest. Dr. Zax had stressed the importance of being still and undisturbed. So far she had not followed any of his advice.

After dinner Doris fell asleep and slept this time without distractions. I, too, slept on her sofa, ready if she needed me. The next morning when Dr. Zax arrived and made his usual house call, I briefed him on the adventures of the previous day. He assured me he would take care of her. He went into her room to find her propped up in bed smiling from ear to ear like the cat that swallowed a canary. He asked, "Doris, what have you been up to?" She replied, "Why, doctor, what do you mean?" He paused and started laughing and asked, "What is this I hear about your dyeing clothes?" We all started laughing, and she agreed to stay in bed from now on.

All of us survived the face-lift, but I think I aged a little. Within a couple of weeks Doris was up and around and more or less back to her routine, but still under restrictions about going out into the sun and not over-exercising. It was my job to make sure she followed the doctor's orders.

Alma finally returned home from her family in Houston. Doris didn't want her to know about either of the operations, and she asked Ruth to invite her mom to go over to her house for a week or so. Doris told her mother she had the flu. Alma was not to come. Fortunately, Alma believed the story, and we kept up the pretense for a while. Eventually, she wanted to visit. The afternoon Alma arrived, Doris wore a long, orange terry robe, a floppy hat to cover most of her head, and dark sun glasses to keep her eyes from showing. Hardly the typical Doris Day outfit, but Alma stayed in the dark that day. Weeks passed, and Doris kept looking in the mirror to see if all of the swelling had gone down. I thought she looked great, but of course, I thought she looked great before the operation. She naturally was more aware of what was done. Dr. Zax was a perfectionist just like his patient, and no scars remained. Life returned to normal at last!

10

Living with "Clara Bixby"

The original plan had me living with Doris for about one month over the Christmas holidays while Nada visited Yugoslavia. Days turned into weeks and weeks into months, but no word from Nada. I began to wonder if she would ever return. One day I received a call from a man asking to speak to Nada. I explained that she went to Yugoslavia. To my surprise, he said he was her husband and hadn't heard from her in weeks. I told Doris, and she was distressed at the news. She would never have hired a married person since she required so much time and service, which would not be appropriate for a wife's lifestyle. Nada had not been honest.

The outlook did not look promising for Nada's return. Still, we decided to wait until we heard from her. One day she phoned to ask about everyone. I questioned her about returning, and she told me she did not want to be a housekeeper anymore, hoping to go into something more stimulating! Young and married, why should she be stuck cleaning someone's home?

It was slowly dawning on me that I was falling into the same pattern, young and cleaning house. Doris required someone to care for many animals and keep her home spotless. I could see myself now in a 24/7 position with her. The more she needed me, the less I saw of friends. She knew I would do anything for her, and I was happy to be with her, especially when she was without help. It was a trade-off, and for the time being I enjoyed this lifestyle. Still, I had passed beyond just being a doting fan to friendship.

And as a friend, I knew I needed a life of my own.

Doris seemed disappointed when I told of my chat with Nada, who was good with the dogs—really the qualification for anyone who walked through her door. So I needed to start calling employment agencies and newspapers to run an ad for a new maid. The lead line appeared in capital letters and bold type, **MUST LOVE DOGS!** Not many people answered, and those who did were real kooks. In daily contact with the agencies, I made it clear that they should carefully screen each applicant to make sure she really liked animals. Otherwise, we would be wasting each other's time. Finally a few apparently better prospects came to interview, with Doris asking me to see them first in the den. If anyone seemed promising, I should buzz her on the intercom, and she would check the person out. What a cross section of applicants: everything from a teeny-bopper to a hooker! Discouraged, Doris decided to call it quits.

Doris knew from her friends that good help was hard to find. She had been spoiled with Kay and Katie, who had stayed for years until age took its toll. In addition, people didn't want to live in any more, and day help came expensive. Doris wanted one person to do all the work in her house; and, of course, the work never was finished. The dogs were an added attraction or distraction, depending on how one looked at it.

Many times Doris would confide, "Marzy, if I didn't have all these dogs, I'd love to take a bungalow up at the Beverly Hills Hotel, and I'd be very comfortable." You could sense the longing in her voice, yet I told myself she had made the decision to place herself with the overwhelming responsibilities of the dogs.

During this time Doris gave me my one-and-only raise—from $140 a week to $165 a week. A lot of people think movie stars pay their secretaries huge salaries, but my work was a labor of love. Unfortunately, I could not bank much of my salary, because I had to keep up my apartment. Since we had no idea when help would be found, I needed a place to stay and store my things. Doris was generous in many ways, but I ran most of the errands with my car and on my gas, and I should have asked for reimbursement, but I was so happy to be with her that the thought never crossed my mind. Sometimes celebrities are not too practical since they become accustomed to things being done for them.

Needless to say, I became adept at all types of non-secretarial jobs: sanding and painting her outdoor furniture, filling holes in the backyard so the dogs did not fall and break their legs, washing windows, driving a 16-foot truck, washing and grooming the dogs, moving furniture, fixing electrical outlets and garbage disposals, setting rat traps because rats nested in the palm trees, and putting up fences. All in addition to daily dusting, sweeping, mopping, vacuuming, and cooking. I was young and single and willing to attempt new things, and that was lucky in the situation.

I will never forget the night it poured rain for hours, and Doris and I went to bed. As soon as I got into my room, I sat on the bed, and it felt wet. I couldn't imagine one of the dogs having an accident since they were good about going outside. All of a sudden I felt a drop of water on my hand and looked up to see water coming in from the ceiling. I jumped up and buzzed Doris. She came in to check it out, and I asked, "Do you have a ladder?" We trudged out to the garage to hunt for the extendable ladder. Her roof was flat, and apparently leaves clogged the drain. We put on slickers, and as she held the ladder, I ventured up and onto the roof, where water stood inches deep. I had a stick and a rake and managed to scrape the leaves aside, allowing the water to rush down. I threw the leaves over the side of the house so as not to have them accumulate again. This was our own version of the usual klutz scene from a Laurel and Hardy movie.

Another time Doris and I walked by her pool near the deep end and noticed one of her chaises at the bottom, tossed by the winds the night before. Doris didn't ask me to dive in and get it, but commented, "I think it's going to rust down there." Later, while she was on the phone, I found extra clothesline and called out to her from the patio. I was going to dive in and retrieve that chair. She called back, saying she did not think I should do that, but if I did, I should be careful. I figured I would at least try once, and if it didn't work, we would call someone. It was early spring and nippy, so I dove in with all my clothes on, wrapped the clothesline around the chair and surfaced with it.

One afternoon Rudy and Schatzie were in the den with me with the doors open. Doris was keeping Biggest, their rival, with her in her bedroom. She walked through the house and peeked in to see me for a minute and then proceeded to the kitchen, apparently forgetting the doors of the den and bedroom were not closed. Naturally the dogs would all rather be with their mom than Aunt Mary Anne, so the two dauxis made their way into the kitchen. All of a sudden I heard Doris screaming to come quickly. She was caught in the middle of another fight among the three warriors. She never wanted the kids to get hurt, so she would put her hand in one dog's mouth to keep him from biting the other. Poor Clara always got it! I came running to help, picked up Biggest by the tail and took him outside. Doris shook from pain and fright, and Rudy bled from head to toe.

Because of Rudy's injuries, Doris asked me to take him immediately to the vet. I put him in my car with the white leather interior. In no time, Rudy shook and splattered the inside of my car with blood. Doris had already phoned the vet, and the assistants awaited our arrival. While the vet sewed up Rudy's injuries, I decided to go to the nearby carwash to have the inside wiped clean. The men at the carwash, noticing that I had fresh blood, still wet, all over the upholstery, questioned me extensively. The situation set off alarms. At first they were reluctant to help the possible murderer—me. But as I explained that I was Doris Day's secretary and told them about the dog altercation at her home, they smiled and took care of me. Poor Rudy had stainless steel stitches on his back and on the tip of his tail. When we returned home, Doris welcomed the injured skirmisher, but she still seemed shaken. She always had an emotional reaction to these battles, and they began to take their toll on her.

One day Bucky, #10, came down with kennel cough. My bedroom became the isolation ward and gradually began to fill up with other dogs who caught this highly contagious ailment. I woke up one morning with a strange cough and buzzed Clara to make an appointment for me with the vet. We both laughed, but I did have a cough. The epidemic made its rounds quickly and never returned. When Doris realized her dogs needed their annual shots, she called her favorite vet, and he and his nurse came to the house. She arranged things in the kitchen for them and brought in one dog at a time. Each was examined and given its shots.

Her kids vied for her attention. Schatzie used to follow Gertie around, and after she left, he took a liking to me and became my shadow. No matter where I went, there came "Thumper." He got this name because any time he saw a human, he would roll over and start thumping his tail on the floor. Doris had at first not wished to share her dogs. She told me not to pay attention to Schatzie. He was hers, but in no time, she changed her mind and seemed glad that the kids seemed to like me, too. After all, I was with them as much as she, if not more. It was not easy to give each the same attention, but we worked hard at it.

Crime seemed to pay at her home: Biggest, my old friend and #11, got to go to meetings and interviews and appeared to be the chosen one in spite of his bad behavior. Doris found that Rudy, the older of the two dauxis, became the real trouble-maker, especially around food. He had to be fed first and kept away from the others. Otherwise, he would eat his dinner and then the food in the other bowls and still be looking for more, heart condition and all. He was so elderly, Alma often said, "Rudy's so old he voted for Lincoln."

Doris frequently ate lunch and dinner in her room at the wicker desk by her bed, and sometimes breakfast if we didn't go to Nate 'N Al's. We had to put the dogs out so she could eat in peace. When I brought Doris a tray of food, halfway through the meal she would see noses pressed against the glass windows, with dog eyes looking longingly at her. She melted and would open the sliding door and let the gang in. It was quite a scene to watch her trying to eat surrounded by half a dozen canines to whom she gave treats and tidbits all through her meal. She complained that I gave her too much food, but I knew much of it went to the dogs, so this way she had enough for all.

One Saturday morning we decided to eat in, and I cooked bacon and eggs and brought over her tray. We put the dogs out as usual, and she sat at the edge of her bed peacefully eating. I went back to the kitchen, and within five minutes she buzzed me in a panic saying, "Come quickly!" I raced over to find her, bleeding and crying, with her breakfast dumped all over the glass top on the desk. She said Rudy had strolled in from the front room and was sitting very nicely and calmly beside her. Remembering she needed salt and not thinking, she left a tempting tray to go to the kitchen in her dressing room.

When she returned, Rudy was straddled between Doris's bed and desk with his back feet on her bed and front paws on the desk. She called out to him to leave it alone. The orders fell on deaf ears, and he continued to consume the breakfast. Seeing that he wasn't going to budge, Doris grabbed a newspaper, rolled it up and tapped him, hoping he would obey. Suddenly, he became ferocious, starting toward her, eyes glowering. Rudy bit her twice in the thigh, and she finally had to get him away like a lion tamer, grabbing a chair and coaxing him out of the room, leaving his mistress bleeding. I asked her why she did not call me as soon as Rudy started acting strangely. "It all happened so quickly and I know, Marzy, if you saw him bite me, you'd probably kill him." I know I would have done something to try to save her before the altercation. But that was Doris—she loved the kids no matter what. Unfortunately, she usually ended up the victim, and she carries the scars to prove it.

Mother's Day of 1973: Mary, Linda, and I took Doris and Alma out to the Magic Pan in Beverly Hills for an early dinner. We had a good time, and Doris, Alma, and I returned home. We followed the usual procedure of Doris's going to her side of the house to let her dogs out. Alma followed, and I went to the kitchen to let my crew out in the side yard. Seconds later Alma rushed into the living room, shouting, "My daughter's finger is coming off!" I raced to Doris's bedroom, and there I found Doris at her sink running water on her bleeding left hand.

"What in the world happened, Clara?" I asked. There was blood all over her camel skirt, the sink, and some furniture. Her ring finger hung by a thread, and she was in such pain that nothing in her medicine chest would help. When she had entered the bedroom, the dogs jumped up to her as usual. As she walked to the doggie door, several got into a fight, and not wanting them to get injured, she reached down to separate the warring dogs, and one or two crunched down on her left hand.

It all happened quickly, and now she needed immediate medical attention. I got her in the car and drove to Mount Sinai Hospital. They did not have an emergency room, so I phoned Doris's personal doctor in Glendale, and he told me not to let anyone touch her until he got a hand surgeon for her. I sat with Doris in the waiting room, while she kept her hand in a bowl with antiseptic solution, which did not alleviate her pain. She looked so pitiful, shaking and crying. I offered her a Valium, and she took it gladly, hoping for relief.

Nine o'clock on Mother's Day evening: doctors were with their families. Out of eight hand specialists in the Los Angeles area, Doris's doctor located only one to take the case. Dr. Nicholudius just happened to be at a dinner party in Palos Verdes and agreed to come, not knowing who his patient was. It took over an hour before he arrived, and all the while Doris limply sat in the dimly lit waiting room. When Nicholudius arrived, he took over like the pro that he was and performed the surgery. By the time he had finished, Doris had twenty stitches on her ring finger.

Doris was confined to bed once again with instructions to keep her left arm elevated. In excruciating pain, even with the pain pills, she was restless. During the following week I had to take her to see Dr. Nicholudius several times. She hated the drive to his downtown LA office. The sights (trash in the streets, vacant buildings, and many homeless wandering aimlessly) along the way depressed her. His office was just around the corner from the famous McArthur Park, made popular by Richard Harris's song of the same name and filled with lost souls. The last time we saw Dr. Nick he told us about an upcoming medical convention he would attend. Since he would be gone for her normal checkup, he would see her when he returned the following week.

A couple days later as I prepared breakfast, I had the radio on in the kitchen. KNX, the big all-news station, was reporting a fatal plane crash. I thought I heard the name Nicholudius. Doris was supposed to see him the next day. The phone rang, and his office informed us about his tragic death, letting us know Doris would be seeing his associate. I was shocked, and I knew Doris would be distressed.

I brought her breakfast on a tray, putting fresh flowers from her garden in a little vase to brighten it up. When I entered, she was sitting up, with head on her knees pulled up close to her body, holding some Kleenex. She was crying and asked me, "Marzy, did you hear the news?" She had heard the same report on TV. The associate took excellent care of her; however, it took months for her to get over the shock of her injury and the sadness of her doctor's untimely death. While her hand improved, she became engrossed in the Watergate hearings and watched gavel to gavel. She did not leave home unless she absolutely had to.

Within days the *National Enquirer* ran a story that Doris's secretary had slammed the car door on the star's finger. My mother sent me a copy of the article, which named me as the cause of her trouble. "Why haven't you told me about this?" Mother demanded. I explained the real story, but I think she was a little skeptical. Mom should have known how much I thought of Doris. I would never have been that careless.

I practiced my nursing skills again, feeling semi-professional, especially at night when I came around with a tray of pills for Doris and her canine kids. Some took heart pills, some liquid medication, and Daisy, the collie, had Dilantin for an epileptic condition. We had a house full of invalids.

In 1973 Doris and I watched Elvis's "Aloha from Hawaii," the first TV program to be beamed around the world by satellite, viewing it in the vacant maid's room off the kitchen. Doris liked some of Elvis's music, and the movie was a major musical event of sorts. As we watched, I told her about riding next to him from Palm Springs back to Los Angeles; I didn't dare tell her we had followed her there the day before.

This year was full of surprises. Doris went to her first and only X-rated movie, *The Last Tango in Paris,* with Billy De Wolfe. He asked her to go to the sexy movie which was a benefit for a charity. Mrs. Jeanne (Dean) Martin chaired the event, along with other Hollywood elites: Mrs. Henry Fonda, Mrs. Harold Robbins, and Gloria Romanoff. The whole town talked about the movie, and no one was sure until the final day if Doris would actually go. Neither she nor Billy could believe what they saw and heard. It bored and disgusted them.

Several weeks after her facelift, Doris asked me to help her streak her hair. Her hairdresser Barbie Lampson was filming, and Doris didn't want to go to a nearby beauty shop. She was afraid a beautician might see the scars on her scalp. Doris knew the color she wanted and had a solution on hand. After she asked me to get the tin foil to do the streaking "just like Barbie did," she put on the cap. I mixed the solution and applied it with the swab, wrapping each strand with tin foil. We followed the directions exactly, kept the solution on the required time, and then started to unveil our production. As we took each strand down, to our shock we saw Doris had a perfect circle of golden hair on her head! The solution must have run together, and the top of her head looked like she wore a golden yamulka. Fortunately, Doris looked good in hats!

One day in early 1973, Doris told me she had received a letter from Jacqueline Susann, the famous writer, whom she did not know. Jackie had been moved to write because of a story Hollywood columnist Rex Reed had written in newspapers nationwide about Doris's interest in animals. Jackie commented that the photo with the article—a profile close-up of her and one of her black poodles—reminded her of Josephine, her pampered poodle, who was now gone. She and her husband, Irving Mansfield, were coming to the coast to supervise the film version of her book *Once Is Not Enough,* and were to stay at the Beverly Hills Hotel up the street. Doris wrote back inviting them to visit when they had settled in.

The two came, and we had a delightful time. Irving was on the quiet side, but Jackie, the lively one, talked a mile a minute. Doris appeared to enjoy their company. I was prepared not to like Jackie, believing since she wrote "trashy" books, her type didn't appeal to me. I believed I would have to put on an act as a gracious talker. Was I wrong! Jackie, soon known as

"Opal" (the nickname Doris gave her), was one of the nicest, most generous people I have ever met. With nothing phony about her, she was always cordial and charming. The Mansfields stayed in a bungalow at the hotel for a few weeks, with Jackie frequently calling Doris to go to lunch or visit. From the beginning, Jackie was determined to find a man to take care of Doris, a gentleman to treat her new friend like Irving treated her, but Doris remained indifferent.

Doris managed to double bandage her hand, cast and all, for the 2nd Annual Actors and Others for Animals Celebrity Fair on June 3, 1973, at the Burbank Studios. The fair was organized to raise money and aid the plight of animals—and gave the attendees a good time. We drove to the studio the day before to check the setup. I designed and put together "Doris Day's Dog House," a booth with items for sale, including coffee cups with her signature on one side and a caricature of Doris on the other. Olive Abbott, Alma's friend and Bud Abbott's sister, manned the dog house. In the booth was fabric with a dog print and other swatches of cloth featuring the Pepsi logo. Fans came from miles around to participate. Many avid Doris Day fans, eager for a firsthand, up-close look at their favorite star, flocked to her trailer. "Please get me in to see Doris." I could identify with that. Once word got out that I was her secretary, eager fans mobbed me, wanting to know if they could meet the star. Doris's booth became one of the most popular on the lot, and people stood in line to buy anything "Doris"!

Doris was autographing programs and photos, which was awkward since she wore that cast to protect her hand. Pepsi stands stood all over the lot because she had contacted Joan Crawford, President of Pepsico, asking if Joan would donate her product for the event, which she gladly did.

Many celebrities worked long, hard hours to pull the event together. Some of those who turned out were: Jacqueline Susann, Kris and Rick Nelson, Jackie Joseph, Jo Anne Worley, Lucie Arnez, David Hartman, Rod McKuen, and Susan Saint James. Jackie sat in the hot sun for hours autographing her books, *Valley of the Dolls* and *Every Night Josephine*. People swarmed around her, and she just kept signing. Doris was impressed with all the time Jackie spent there. At the right moment, Doris moved to the stage for the live auction. As one of the highlights, she auctioned off one of her bikes to the highest bidder. A record crowd showed up to help the cause, raising $70,000.

Following the bazaar, Doris began preparing for her first dog food commercial for General Foods. They had developed a new line called "Gaines Supreme." The advertising company, Ogilvy and Mather, would pay her $175,000, and Gaines planned to put out a cool million for her spots over the next couple of years. Doris was a natural, for this, and the filming date was set for June 16th at her home. The script did not arrive until the day before the filming, so we read lines in the early evening, Doris in her night-gown propped up in bed and I standing near her desk. We did not want to stay up too late because the crew would arrive at 6:00 AM.

About 6:00 PM the phone rang. Irving Mansfield began pleading with Doris to come to Jackie's party for the opening of *Once Is Not Enough*. When she hung up, she told me Irving had reminded her that Jackie came to the Actors and Others bazaar and sent and autographed hundreds of books for the animal cause. Now he insisted Doris be at the event to promote Jackie's own cause—her book. Reluctantly, she asked him to send someone to pick us up in one hour.

You never saw two people get out of night gowns and into formal eve-ning wear faster than we did. Jackie's agent, Jay Allen, picked us up, but Doris kept telling me before we left, "Marzy, we're only staying for one hour because we both have to be up early tomorrow for the commercial." I didn't care how long we stayed; I was just happy to be going.

Doris wore a chic, apple green jersey pant suit, and Jackie dressed in a bright orange flowing gown; the two blended beautifully. All sorts of people gathered, even some from a nearby book convention. Jackie grabbed Doris immediately for publicity shots with her, and they began circulating and posing. I kept waiting for Doris to give me the high sign that we would leave, but her hour turned into two and then three. Finally at 2:00 AM Jay Allen called me and said Doris was ready. Exhausted, we left while the oth-ers kept on celebrating with merriment and laughter.

We slept fast, as Doris would say, and were up by 5:30 AM. Barbie and Connie, and the seamstress Joy were due at 6:00 AM. The rest of the TV crew, numbering about 40, were to arrive at 6:30 to set up for the shoot. It was a sunny day, and the backyard was transformed into a sound stage with people and electronic equipment all over. It was hard for me to understand how it took so many hands to produce a 60-second and a 30-second com-mercial. Armed with my movie camera and the still camera to capture the behind-the-scenes action, I felt the fan in me click back into gear. Doris looked gorgeous in a blue, long-sleeve blouse and fawn-colored slacks. She was not wearing her cast, and only a band-aid appeared on her hand in most photos. The backyard never looked as good as it did that day, with red geraniums standing tall and brilliant against the white wood fence.

The commercial began with Doris and five of her dogs, Daisy, Bambi, Muffy, Bucky, and Bubbles. Then the crew, Doris, and the dogs started walking and running to her patio, where two "actor" dogs waited to do their part. None of our dogs ate the food in the commercial, only the actors. Filming was delayed at least two hours because as the main camera rolled on the cement across the pool from her, a lens fell into the pool. The crew had no replacement and had to find another. People stood around waiting, and finally the new lens arrived and was securely placed on the main camera, and shooting continued.

Since the dog food came in three flavors—chicken, liver, and lamb—Doris spoke of each flavor. On the last take, she surprised everyone with the comment, "All my dogs like the Beef Gaines Supreme, but Muffy and my secretary, Mary Anne, like the Chicken Gaines Supreme!" The last of the crew left around 9:30 with everyone pleased with the day's work. We were scheduled to see the rushes in two days at a screening room at the Beverly Hills Hotel.

Two days later Terry came to pick us up to view the rushes. He was eager for the commercial to be successful for his mother's sake and for the money. The commercial and product would appear in two test city markets, Denver and Miami, and then nationwide. Unfortunately, because the time was late 1973 and early 1974, and the price per can around fifty cents, most people in that slightly light market couldn't pay that much. Sales were not good, although it had an acceptable aroma, unlike most canned dog food. Dogs loved it, but the deal did not take off. Doris received at least five cases of the variety of flavors for every month for a year, which the dogs appreciated. I never did hear whether Doris's comments about my love of the chicken version ended up on the cutting room floor in the final version or not.

Doris spent much time in 1973 with the Mansfields at their bungalow at the hotel. Jackie and Irving knew everyone and "the" places to go, and Doris used to feel a little foolish when she came from a luncheon or dinner with them. They dropped names, but, of course, they knew many celebrities and truly had dealings with everyone they talked about. Doris returned dizzy after lunch at the Polo Lounge, the fancy dining spot at the hotel. It was "business, business, business" for Jackie and Irving. "It boggles the mind,"

Doris would say. "They just really talk about business, and who cares?" That was typical Doris and probably typical, too, of Jackie and Irving. With their worlds far apart, they still complemented each other, creating a strong bond among the three.

But Doris frequently came home shaken after an evening with Jackie and Irving for another reason: Jackie was a reckless driver. "Mary Anne, we went through so many red lights. The next time I go with them, I want you to drive," she said. Being a New Yorker, Irving never got used to LA streets, so Jackie drove their rented car. The next evening Doris was invited to dinner with them, she called the hotel to say I would drive over to get them in a few minutes. But the doorman told her, "The Mansfields just left, Miss Day. They will be at your home in a couple of minutes." When Jackie arrived, Doris insisted I drive. "Park the car," she said. Jackie, paying no attention called out, "Oh, come on, Clara. Don't you trust my driving? Get in, we're running a little late." Doris reluctantly got in, and they drove off. I prayed all would make it home safely, and they did.

In spite of all the business talk, Doris never really felt like a fifth wheel with Jackie and Irving but looked forward to their visits to LA. They got her out of the house, something she needed. I kept assuring her "go ahead and have a good time. I'll take care of the dogs and the house. You don't have to worry about a thing." One afternoon Jackie invited Doris, Rack (an interior decorator friend of Doris who knew the Mansfields years before in New York), and me to join her at the Polo Lounge to have a drink. We saw Jackie around 3:00 PM in a booth at the back, and she waved us over. As the four of us sat chatting away, I felt like I was at a soda shop with my high school friends, despite the fact that I was at least 22 years younger than these "girls." Jackie kept saying, "I've got to find a man like Irving to take care of you, Clara." Doris would wave her off. "Oh, Opal, I'm fine."

The lounge was not crowded that afternoon, and while we enjoyed a leisurely drink, Jackie surveyed the place. Suddenly she spotted the actor best known for his starring role in the hit TV show, "The Fugitive," David Janssen, at a corner booth with some men. He was going to co-star in the movie version of *Once Is Not Enough*. You could see her mind working. Suddenly she said to Doris, "Clara, get up and go to the ladies room." Jackie wanted to make sure David saw the "new" Clara in her form-fitting sweater and slacks. Doris looked surprised and promptly replied, "But I don't have to go." Finally it became obvious what Jackie was trying to do: she didn't care where Doris went as long as she got up and passed through the lounge, making a grand entrance when she returned. Jackie told her to go walk in the lobby for a while—anything—so that Janssen would notice, but Doris was too reticent to do that.

We sipped our bloody bulls, when all of a sudden, David Janssen himself came to our table. You could see the gleam in Jackie's eyes as Clara and David began to chat. He was a real charmer and so good looking, fresh off his recent TV series "Harry O." It must have been through Jacqueline that David got Doris's phone number, and not long after he called to ask her out.

She told me David would arrive about five, and I needed to visit with him until she was ready. Almost at the stroke of five the doorbell rang. I had most of the dogs scattered about—only two in the living room with me. I opened the door, and there he was, handsome as ever with his off-white Rolls Royce convertible in the driveway. I invited him in, and we sat at the cherry wood bar, which George Montgomery, Dinah Shore's husband, had made for the Melchers years before. It had been strictly a soda and ice cream fountain in those non-drinking days with many chocolate sundaes served. This evening, however, we had drinks and chatted about anything and everything from Linda Lovelace to this being the "year of the uglies," as he called it, referring to strange outfits he saw at the lounge.

David started telling me something about his feet and proceeded to take off both of his leather boots and socks, leaving him standing in his bare feet. That's when Doris came through the door with a look of surprise. "What are you doing?" she asked. Neither one of us knew what to answer. She looked radiant in a powder-blue blouse with a chamois-colored pantsuit, casual and elegant. She smelled divine, too, wearing her "Mr. Guy" specialty perfume. As they left, she told me she would not be out late. We said goodbye, and I got the dogs arranged and then watched TV before going to sleep. I thought I would know when she came home because all the dogs would bark. We had canine radar at that house, and it worked every time.

I dozed off and awoke. Looking at my watch, I saw it was 11:30 PM. She should be home any time. I dozed off again, and I looked at my watch at 2:30 AM. I had not heard barking. Where was she? I didn't dare call her, but was getting concerned at this late hour since she had not planned to stay out. I dozed off again and then looked at my watch at four, and still no barking. You would have thought I was waiting for my teenage daughter.

At about 4:30 AM I heard the commotion that told me she came home. The door slammed shut in the living room as I heard his car drive off, and I got up to meet her in the hallway. I do not know if I surprised her more or if she surprised me, but she looked sick. "Oh, Marzy, I feel awful. It must have been something I ate. I spent most of the evening in the bathroom and then on his sofa. I was so sick. His oriental maid had fixed something that was out of this world, but, oh, what an evening! I got sick on the wine, threw up, and fell asleep on the couch. Finally, at 4:00 AM, he nudged me and said, 'Doris, I think it is time to take you home.'" The next morning Jackie called hoping for good news, but got only the discouraging details.

Her birthday cake was deco-
rated with Doris's favorite
flowers—daisies for an April
3, 1972, birthday party.

Doris met Kris Nelson (right cut off) and their twin boys Gunnar
and Matthew (Rick Nelson was their father) at the second Actors and
Others for Animals event in 1973.

Alma, the star's mother, accompanied her to Musso Frank's restaurant in 1973 with a four-legged friend.

Posing perkily at the Actors and Others for Animals event in June, 1974, at Burbank studios, is one of America's perennial animal lovers.

11

Doris Flies to London

I'll never forget the night in 1973 at the Hamburger Hamlet on Sunset Boulevard, just at the edge of Beverly Hills, when Doris made an historic announcement. After many years of suffering from "fear of flying," she would be jetting to London.

Jacqueline Susann and Irving had invited her, her mom, Rack and me to dinner at the Hamlet, a place Jacqueline really liked. It was Sunday night, and Doris again insisted I drive. We picked up the Mansfields at the hotel and made the short trip to the restaurant for an evening filled with good conversation and good American food. We ordered their famous hamburgers and tried Jackie's favorite cocktail, a bloody bull, a bloody mary with bouillon and Worcestershire.

During the conversation, Jackie announced she and Irving were leaving soon for London in September for two weeks. *Once Is Not Enough* was now out, and she was taking the book on a publicity tour. When Rack asked, "When are you leaving?" Jackie gave her the dates, and Rack exclaimed, "My mother and I are going to be there the very same time." They began talking about how they could connect.

Since Rack had known the Mansfields in New York, they were comfortable with each other. Comparing notes, they decided they would like to fly over together. More discussion followed, and all eyes fell on Doris. The chorus asked together, "Well?" Doris answered, "Don't look at me. I don't fly. Clara is not going." She said she had not flown since the 1950s when she made *The Man Who Knew Too Much*. She would never forget that last bumpy plane ride. The group spent the entire evening encouraging her. "You need to go to London and start to fly again," Jackie insisted. Before the night ended, Doris confidently announced, "Yes, I'll fly to London." "You'll love it, I'll guarantee it," Jackie told her. The dinner came to an end with Doris and Jackie's splitting a huge tin-roof sundae, a giant gooey concoction big enough for two.

We climbed into Doris's Imperial: Opal seated directly behind me, Irving in the middle, and Rack in the back passenger seat. After having two bloody bulls, I felt giddy. All of a sudden I asked Jackie, "Opal, why do you write such dirty books?" Doris, sitting next to me with her mom on the passenger side, gave me a gentle elbow in the ribs. But Opal was patient, asking, "Marzy, have you ever read any of them?" To which I replied, "I would never waste my time reading that trash."

"What have I done?" I thought. "I'm kissing my job good-bye," but nothing was mentioned about my remarks then or later. We all must have been a little high, and no one took me seriously.

As the time approached for the trip, Doris began shopping, something she rarely cared to do. Department stores were zones of avoidance for her, but this time she looked forward to a new adventure. Previously she always asked Connie to select a variety of clothes, bring them to her home, and let her choose. She did not have to rush around shopping for herself.

Now I went with Doris from store to store up and down Wilshire Boulevard in Beverly Hills, spending hours looking for the right garments for London events. Very selective, almost frugal in her buying, Doris purchased only what she needed. She wanted to get special gowns for the boat because they planned to return to New York on the *Queen Elizabeth II*. While we were in Saks to purchase shoes, a clerk asked Doris to sign her name, pressing extra hard on the charge slip. After Doris checked and signed it, the girl said, "Thank you, Miss Day, for your autograph. I would get fired if I asked you for one, so I slipped in an extra piece of carbon to have a souvenir." Doris smiled at the beaming admirer.

For a non-shopper Doris acclimated herself well, breezing through every store, checking out everything, picking up garments, holding them up to herself at the mirror, I following one step behind. She hated waiting for packages and preferred trying on clothes at home. So as she went on to the next department, I waited to gather her parcels. It reminded me of a scene from *Breakfast At Tiffany's* where Audrey Hepburn goes on a marathon shopping spree.

Jacqueline's trademark sign was the Egyptian "ankh," one of the world's oldest known symbols, and Doris found an elegant and delicate gold ankh ring at Saks. She loved a solid gold ankh and chain Jacqueline had presented to her the previous Christmas and decided this would be the perfect complement. After she bought the ring and had it sized, she noticed a costume pin that reminded us both of her little dauxi, Schatzie. She knew how much I loved him, and she bought me that pin. Today I enjoy wearing it because it reminds me of both my two-legged and my four-legged friends on Crescent Drive.

Many last-minute shopping sprees followed before the big day. Doris had to think about luggage. She told me she hated her suitcases. "Someday I'll get something I really like, maybe in French blue. Marty was always making deals for everything, and I ended up with dark brown luggage." I could sense this was true not only about luggage but about other things. Doris never talked much about Marty, but when she did, it did not put him in a good light. But this story about the luggage surprised me. It reinforced my feeling that, although she was the bread-winner of the family and a top box-office attraction, Marty controlled the purse strings and her life. I couldn't believe this famous, beloved lady did not have something as simple as suitcases she really wanted. Even I, with my limited budget, had picked out my own luggage over the years. It made me sad since she would occasionally complain about things or conditions in her life, but then put up with them and do nothing to make a change. Doris finally selected luggage at a boutique shop in Beverly Hills just down from Nate 'N Al's. It was practical; she said she would look around for what she really wanted at a later date.

The big day arrived. Rack hired a limousine to drive her own mother, Doris, Alma, herself, and me to the airport. Our friend David Knox followed in his station wagon with all the luggage. We met at the TWA Ambassador Club, where VIPs waited in pampered style. Doris was very calm during the ride, which surprised us. She seemed eager to fly. We relaxed with a cocktail, and Tom Stout, the TWA man who handled celebrities, came over to greet us and make sure all last minute arrangements were handled with ease. The only other celebrity in the club was Danny Kaye, who spoke briefly and sat down again.

Time passed quickly. Doris had a new outfit for the flight and looked attractive in beige plaid slacks and blue sweater set with a denim blue cap, wearing her ankh ring and chain especially for the Mansfields. Soon we were at the gate saying our good-byes. Doris hugged and kissed her mother, and then kissed me, saying, "I'll miss you, Marzy, and I love you. Take care of yourself, Nana, and my babies." With a little crying and more good-byes, the three Beverly Hills ladies flew off to New York aboard a 747 to meet the rest of their party and fly on to London town.

Alma and I rode back with David, then waited for a call from the travelers. Jackie and Irving had made a reservation for the three at the Navarro Hotel half a block from their Central Park South apartment. When Doris called that night, she told us they all hated the Navarro and had decided to stay at the Park Lane instead. Billy De Wolfe was also in town, and they were going to get together for dinner and a festive evening.

Alma spent the following two weeks at Doris's home with me. Although the boss was away, there was to be no vacation. I had a to-do list a mile long. All employed by Doris worked when she was out of town; everything on the specialized lists created by her needed immediate attention. But it was easier to accomplish things with Doris away because, when she was there, it was so easy to get distracted by her without getting any one thing completed. One list had several important items, and by the last item, she wrote, "Marzy, by the time you get to the end of this list, I'll probably be home again!"

Doris wrote from London, saying she and Rack had awakened at 4:00 AM to find a rainy day. They were staying in a comfortable hotel, located on a scenic path, which they could see from their window. As she had expected, she had enjoyed the plane trip. Jacqueline was starting on her heavy book tour the next day, so she and all the rest of the party had retired early. She closed by saying,

> Going to get dressed soon. Just wanted to say Hi. Tell Terchy [Terry] I send love and stay well, Nana, and on your diet!!! Give Lin and Mary my love, too, and everyone. I'm loving my trip and Rack and I giggle constantly. She and Rose [Rack's Mom] send love along with mine. Clara"

Another letter followed shortly. She began by telling us:

All is well here (a great city) and now we've decided to go to Paris on Thursday night, spend Friday there and home that night. Back to London, I mean. We'll rent a car and driver there and see the city, have some great food (I can feel the burps now). Oh, oh, I'll need Calso and that's it. No buying there—it is so expensive we hear.

Then she went on to say that she still had not adjusted to the time change, but was soldiering on. She had invited the London Doris Day Society up for champagne, about 12 members. And she was impressed with the way Londoners treated their dogs. She closed by saying she missed all of us and that she would send cards from Paris.

She had seemed to be enjoying the trip and her companions, but the scene changed quickly. A tearful Doris phoned me from Paris. With Alma out, I took the call. She hated Paris and said she had not wanted to go, but she didn't want to stay alone in London, either.

"What about the Mansfields?" I asked. "They left for New York yesterday, and I didn't want to stay in London alone so I went with Rack and her mom to Paris." The original plans seemed to be scrapped with the threat of bad sailing weather. Obviously, the three Beverly Hill ladies were not going to sail on the QE II.

So Doris, Rack, and Rack's mother finally returned, exhausted, to Los Angeles on a polar flight from London. Alma and I went to LAX to meet them and could see the weary women going through customs. We waited a long time to get them home to learn all about the trip. It was dark when we arrived, but Doris still saw the huge hanging banner I made and nailed between two posts in front of her home, WELCOME HOME, MOMMY, in foot-high lettering and doggie prints all around as a border. I also tacked a carpet of red flannel to the steps and stretched it to the door to welcome her. Pleased, she asked me to keep it up for a couple of days.

To our surprise her first words inside the door were, "I hated the trip, but loved the plane ride." Doris, now an experienced flyer, told us how much she enjoyed 747s: the food, the service, the whole flight in general. But not only had she never caught up on sleep, but also when the group did everything together, as they constantly did, she felt like she was at a girls' camp. She went on to say that Irving would call in the morning and say, "We'll do something, and then we'll have lunch," and then the gang would all end up doing something else. Planning always went out the door.

Doris and Rack wanted to rent a car and drive through the English countryside, anything but what they actually did. Paris was the worst. Maxim's, the posh restaurant, proved expensive, with dinner for three coming to nearly $100, and the cab fare to the airport was outrageous. People's body odor awful, especially French people's. Doris was fastidious about cleanliness; that breach of hygiene got to her. The only day they planned to go "on the town," she decided she didn't want to go, but Rack was on one of her shopping sprees.

The three went into a big department store, so crowded that in order to get a place to sit down, Doris went to the wig department where there were some chairs. She sat and felt she had to try on some of the products. "And I ended up with a dumb blonde wig, too," she wailed. The clerk putting a wig on Doris, waving her hands all around and under Doris's nose, had such terrible BO that Doris ended up buying it just to get rid of the smelly woman. Doris bought Mary, Linda, and me each a stuffed dog that she picked up at the London airport. She brought her mom a pretty scarf. We were pleased to be remembered.

The next morning Doris asked her mom and me to join her at Nate 'N Al's for breakfast. I sensed she had been doing a lot of thinking during the night and had something on her mind, so we sat attentively. She told us she felt sure Jackie and Irving had asked her to go just to help promote Jackie's book. I had not suspected that, but the more Doris talked, the more obvious it became that they had wanted to use her celebrity status to enhance the promotional effort. She had believed ulterior motives lurked behind the trip from the beginning, but had hoped for the best.

The more Doris talked about how she thought Jackie used her, the more upset I became. When I returned to her home, I was so upset with Opal that I found the book, *Every Night Josephine,* which she had autographed to me at the Actors and Others for Animals bazaar, and threw it out. Much later I realized how stupid that was.

Gradually stories and photos of Doris and Jackie surfaced in all the newspapers and movie magazines. A piece in Radie Harris's column stated, "The only thing that Doris Day sent out for in her hotel room in London was an iron." That information could only have come from Jacqueline. For some time, a feud went on between them, at least in Doris's mind on the west coast. The friendship remained strong, however, and soon the London episode was relegated to the past.

12

Clara Bixby and Billy De Wolfe

To tell this important aspect of Doris's life, we need to go back to one day late in March, 1971, when I was still in the apartment with Mary. I breakfasted with Doris, having arrived at Martha Randall's about the same time as she. I still used crutches, but drove my car. During the course of our chat, Doris spoke about Billy De Wolfe. We had never met, but I always enjoyed seeing him on TV and in the movies.

Not only was Billy her co-star in two early Warner films, *Tea for Two,* 1950, and *Lullaby of Broadway,* 1951, but also one of her close pals. She told the story of a trip with Connie to Palm Springs for a couple of days. They did not stay at Kaye Ballard's home because Kaye had only two bedrooms, but they found nearby accommodations. Billy came down to "take care of her" with no idea what he was getting into.

Doris announced the parameters of the stay: Billy had to find his own lodging. "You're not going to sleep in the living room, for heaven's sake, and, furthermore, if I feel like running around in my nightgown and robe, I want to feel free to do that, so you'll have to stay at the Whispering Waters or somewhere else."

"Mr. De Wolfe always stays at the best places," he announced solemnly. When he arrived at Doris's overly busy quarters, he exclaimed, "This is a crazy house." Doris described her phone calls in the morning: "He'd call from his hotel, and I'd say, 'Now what time are you coming over?' He'd say, 'Well, I was just going to take a little sun!'" Doris would ask, "When you come, will you stop at the market?" She always had lists of things she needed, especially when not at home.

"What I go through!" he would complain dramatically. "Now, what do you want? What would you have done if I had not come down here?"

"We were constantly calling him, 'Hey, Billy, when you come, would you pick up two quarts of milk and some dog food and some French bread?' He was down there for three days, and he had only two hours of sun. Poor Billy, he was running back and forth continually picking up things for us."

Finally Billy said, "I'm going home to sit by my pool so I can have some sun." He had lived for many years at the Ravenswood in Hollywood, occupying that apartment all the time he worked at Paramount. It was owned by Mae West, who lived just below. Later, when I was invited into Doris's world, I could see that she really loved Billy as a brother, a good man, a dear and generous person.

Doris once told me Billy often questioned her about why he was never signed to work with her after those first two films. In later years he played Mr. Jarvis, Doris's nosey, but lovable, neighbor on "The Doris Day Show." But there were no movie jobs with her. He'd ask me if I thought he would have been good in some of her later hits. He would point out certain characters and parts that would have been perfect: Terry Thomas's role in *Where Were You When The Lights Went Out?* Or the roles Tony Randall played in the three Doris Day-Rock Hudson comedies, or perhaps the role Paul Lynde played in *Send Me No Flowers?* Billy thought he would have been a natural for each of these. He figured Marty must have been behind his never working with Doris. But why? After Marty died in the late 60s, Billy was happy to be asked to play the part of Mr. Jarvis on TV, and the fans loved him.

Doris never liked to watch her old movies on TV. However, if either of the films that she and Billy did together was playing, Billy would call, and they would spend hours on the phone making comments on the movie. Doris said she hated her hair in those early films and despised those "dreadful dresses." She alleged Wardrobe used the same dress for the entire movie, only changing the color. Billy would comment, "But oh, Clara, I look absolutely adorable."

I witnessed one of these phone-critique sessions one evening about 7:00 PM. With dinner over and the dogs quiet, the phone rang. Billy informed Doris that *Lullaby of Broadway* was on. Doris was propped up in a nightgown in her bed with one hand holding the phone and the TV remote in the other. Finally she got to the right channel, and the two began their typical gabfest.

And how had Doris attained the name of "Clara Bixby"? It had become her nickname while they were filming *Lullaby of Broadway*. She became "Clara" to him when he spotted an ad in the newspaper saying, "Clara Bixby Lectures Tonight." She said he always gave his favorite people funny names that didn't fit them at all. It stuck, and some of her best friends called her "Clara," and at times during the period I was with her, she even signed letters that way. One day Doris asked me to order new collars and ID tags for her kids. I ordered 12, 11 for the dogs and one for her—with the name "Clara" on it with her address and phone number. She got a big laugh out of that and wore it once on her show.

Billy used to escort Doris to many parties, often to Kaye Ballard's home or to Betty White and Allen Ludden's house. White was a star of "The Mary Tyler Moore Show" and "Golden Girls," and Ludden game show host for the popular "Password" during the 70s. Billy often spoke of a particular evening at the Luddens. After dinner Doris spotted a comfortable couch. She asked if she could sit there and promptly fell sound asleep for the evening. Hours later Billy tapped her on the shoulder saying, "Clara, wake up. It's time to go home." Doris often fell asleep when she went to parties or even when she entertained at home. If tired, she thought nothing of making herself comfortable, sleeping in the living room for a while. She relaxed easily, and little cat naps seemed to perk her up instantly.

Billy shared her love of animals, and on several occasions he accompanied her when she spoke out for animal rights.

Now more detail on Billy's and Doris's adventure to the X-rated movie, *The Last Tango in Paris,* starring Marlon Brando. Since it was a benefit, Billy arrived in an extra-long, black shiny limousine. He looked dapper in his tuxedo, and Doris wore a long, beige lace evening gown with a cape.

We saw some of the coverage on the 10:00 PM news, but were anxious to hear from our two stars what really went on. When Doris got in, she told me, "The two of us were absolutely quiet in the theater. It was boring, running on and on. There were parts that should have been edited in a better way. I'm surprised at Brando for doing this one." At the dinner following the movie, Doris had gone around to all of the tables picking up leftovers so she could come home with doggie bags. She performed scavenger service for leftover meats even in the finest restaurants.

At an earlier date Billy and his nephew, Tom Ireland, visiting from Ft. Lauderdale, double-dated with Doris and me. He was about my age, and Billy thought "we two young folks" should go to Lawry's with them. Billy came in his Clara Cadillac to pick us up. We rode to the famous Lawry's restaurant on La Cienega Boulevard, arriving and being seated quickly. The waitress took our orders. Then Clara announced she wanted to go to the powder room, and I thought I would too.

Tom asked Billy for directions to the men's room. None of us had any money, so each one asked Billy for money for the attendants. Billy sat there alone. When we returned, he told us the waitress came over to him and asked, "What happened to your party, Mr. De Wolfe?"

"They all deserted me for the washrooms, and I even had to give them money to pee."

Billy loved visiting Clara and relaxing on her newly re-upholstered, over-stuffed, daisy-print couch. He would comment, "Clara, the estate looks lovely." To which she would reply, "What estate? This is my home." Billy loved the kids and always had his trunk full of treats. Muffy, or Myra, as he would call her, was his favorite. He admired the fact that Muffy acted lady-like and regal. The dog went wild when Uncle Billy arrived.

Billy loved all of Doris's dogs, but he only tolerated Rudy, the old dauxi. Doris, however, insisted that he give just as much love to Rudy as he gave the others. When they would talk on the phone, Billy used to say, "Tell Myra 'Hi' for me." And Doris would ask, "Who else do you want to be re-membered to?" And he then went down the entire list, purposely leaving out Rudy's name. She would come back with, "You're missing somebody." And then he'd pause and in a deep, droll voice say, "Oh, yes, say hello to R-U-D-Y." He made Doris laugh long and loud.

When Doris and the Mansfields visited New York preparing to go to London, Billy happened to be in the city. Doris begged him to go with them to London. He was not prepared to leave on such short notice, so he returned to Los Angeles. During the time of the London trip, he called me and said he was going to check himself into UCLA hospital for some tests. His persis-tent cough wasn't getting any better. Confidentially, he requested that when Doris returned home and asked about him, I should not tell her he was in the hospital. "Tell her I went to Santa Barbara," he begged. I agreed and didn't say a word until he decided to give her the information himself.

He was in and out of the hospital in a couple of days. Two months later, when he had to go in again for more tests, Doris asked if we might drive him. As a proud man, he hesitated, but finally agreed. We were the only ones privy to his condition. He told the switchboard operator at the Ravenswood that he was out of town.

Doris asked to meet privately with his doctor. He had no immediate family, except for his nephew in Florida, so we stood in. Doris and I were shattered when the surgeon told us, "Billy is not going to make it." Billy had an inoperable tumor, and nothing could be done for him. The surgeon agreed to wait to break the news to him.

Doris was a very spiritual person even though she did not attend church or profess a structured religion. Her former practice of Christian Science had given her a conviction that healing could occur spiritually, that God could heal. She had watched TV evangelist Kathryn Kuhlman's healing crusades with great interest and felt strongly that this might be the answer for Billy. So she called Miss Kuhlman's office, requesting a private audience for her and Billy as soon as possible. We would go the following Sunday to the Kuhlman Miracle Crusade at the Shrine Auditorium and see the healer privately following the service. Doris was afraid Billy might resist, but to her surprise, he was eager. He, too, hoped for a miracle.

When we arrived, about five-thousand people had gathered, hoping for help, and an usher escorted us to a secluded area in the balcony. Billy was so weak he could hardly make it up the stairs. In no time we recognized a familiar voice. Just in front of us sat June Allyson with a friend, also hoping for a miracle. Doris introduced us, and we had a brief chat before the service. The services brought back memories of watching Oral Roberts with my brother John when we were kids. We used to laugh when Oral would get so worked up and shout, "Heal, heal," to the poor soul hoping for improvement. But this time I took the service seriously. It was similar in some ways to the Roberts service, with a lot of energy in the room and people ready to experience miracles. So were we. We really needed one this time. All eyes focused on Kathryn Kuhlman as she prayed and paced back and forth on the stage. The music was soothing, and one by one people came up to pray with her and be healed.

Billy breathed heavily, but the service was inspiring, and at the moment when the congregation sang a soft and prayerful "Alleluia" with the choir on stage, we were all deeply moved. Doris and I sat on either side of

Billy, and, while most of the congregation stood, we still sat, not wishing for him to exert himself. Suddenly he decided to stand, so we got him up. Weak as he was, he put his arms around us. We stood close, propping him up, feeling his body shaking. Suddenly a feeling of energy ran through my body, a feeling I will never forget or be able to describe. When he put his arm around me, something happened.

Following the service we went to see Miss Kuhlman for a private visit in her dressing room, holding Billy up as we made it down the stairway. Doris stood by him and held his hands while Miss Kuhlman prayed. I watched and prayed, too, hoping for healing. I think Billy knew he was not doing well, but Doris and I did not discuss his condition with him. Miss Kuhlman was gracious and spoke privately to him, then we left for home. A couple of days later Billy checked himself into UCLA hospital in Westwood.

On March 4, 1974, Doris received a call from the hospital to tell us Billy had a blood clot. We needed to come right away. By the time we arrived that evening, we found Billy in his private room in severe pain with oxygen and all sorts of tubes in his body and machines working over him. We tried to hold back tears as we witnessed our friend in such a deplorable state. His phone rang, and he reached over to answer, but he couldn't breathe, much less talk. I slipped out of the room and went to the nurses' station to ask if they would hold all of his calls because it was obvious he was in no condition to be talking on the phone. I wondered, Did he have a private duty nurse? The nurses said, "No, he does not." I pulled Doris aside to tell her, and she rushed to the nurses' station and signed for a private-duty nurse to be at his side from then on.

We returned to do some simple care for him. Doris gently rubbed some lotion on his legs, which seemed to soothe him. I told him with all of his tubes, I thought he looked like an astronaut ready to take off into space. He still had spirit, kicking his legs high into the air, trying to show how agile he was. Dancing was the vehicle he used to enter show business in the 1930s.

We stepped out of the room to the library across the hall so we could wait until the nurses finished working with him. While we were eating, the doctor on the floor came over. "It would be a blessing if he went tonight so that this horrible disease doesn't take its toll for months to come." Doris and I broke down. She decided to phone some of Billy's closest friends to tell them to come. Finally his door opened, and we entered Billy's room. He looked up and seemed pleased we were still there and would stay. Billy's friends began to gather in the hall, and Doris told him they were standing outside his door. He seemed agitated that people would see him in this condition, as he was a private man. He said he only wanted Doris and me, so the others left. It got late, and he told us to go home and get some rest. Obviously, he did not know the seriousness of his condition.

I no longer lived with Doris, but this night she wanted me to stay with her. I went to my apartment to get clothes, make-up, and other items. Doris and I sat up and talked for a while in her living room. Since Alma occupied my former bedroom, Doris brought me some linens, and I slept on the sofa in the living room. When the phone awakened me, I knew the call was about Billy. The buzzer came on, and a tearful Doris told me, "Billy is gone." Morning came too quickly with the news on TV and radio, and the phone never stopped ringing with people expressing their sympathy. Even the ringing made her think of Billy, because she used to pick it up and sometimes call him four or five times a day.

As his representatives, the following day we had to meet with the City Administrator to go through Billy's apartment. Tom flew in from Florida and handled arrangements for his services in Wollaston, Massachusetts, where Billy had been born. Over the years Doris had lost many friends, but Billy was unique. His loss took its toll. Everything reminded her of him: her dogs, especially Muffy, and even the Dewar's White Label he cherished.

And what about Kathryn Kuhlman's prayers? Perhaps one was answered: the doctor's hope Billy would not suffer further. He went before the worst occurred. Losing Billy proved hard on all who knew Billy De Wolfe, but especially for Clara Bixby.

Miss Day and Miss Susann split a whole giant sundae at Hamburger Hamlet in 1973.

Billy De Wolfe was often at Doris's house. Here he is with Muffy dog in October, 1972.

Doris was always laughing when her former co-star came to visit.

Dapper Mr. De Wolfe often escorted Doris to events. They're "on the town" for The Last Tango in Paris *benefit.*

13

The Other Men in Her Life

America's big-screen sweetheart in the 50s and 60s—chased in the movies and caught by many of Hollywood's top leading men like Clark Gable, Rock Hudson, James Garner, Cary Grant, Jimmy Stewart, James Cagney, and a host of others—was a different person from the woman who lived virtually isolated in Beverly Hills. Movie critic Rex Reed categorized her as among the genius recluses who chose not to connect with any Hollywood group—elusive stars like Loretta Young, Barbara Stanwyck, and Katharine Hepburn. As far as the men in her life, Doris in the mid-1970s was often quoted as saying, "I don't ever think I would get married again. I'd rather live with someone."

None of the three marriages prior to 1976 could be classified as happy. Still, Doris recalled that her first husband, trombonist Al Jordan, "left me with a wonderful son Terry." From her second husband, saxophonist George Weidler, "I got into Christian Science." As far as her third husband, Marty Melcher, Doris said he was more of a father figure to both her and Terry. In the early 60s she told Marty she wanted a divorce, and he briefly moved out. However, their lawyer, Jerry Rosenthal, insisted that a legal split was not possible because their money matters were too complicated. So Doris remained with Marty until he died April 19, 1968.

After his death Doris remained more or less in solitude. She rarely went to parties and rarely had parties; she said it wasn't easy to entertain with all the dogs. Some wondered if that was an excuse. Billy served as her date when she had to appear at some function, but she did not mind being alone. She didn't want to depend on her son, now married to Melissa Whittaker, but one night she did just that. Rod McKuen was throwing a party, and Terry wanted her to go. He picked her up, and she seemed to have "high hopes" of meeting someone interesting. But, when she came home, she commented, "There's no future there."

The one exciting affair she experienced during those 70s years I had a small part in. Since she mentioned this event in her autobiography, I feel I can touch on it. During her final year of "The Doris Day Show," she became involved with a co-star, an attractive actor whom she had known for years. By no means a newcomer to the Hollywood scene, he ranked high on her list, and she was delighted that they would be doing a few shows together, which led to a more intimate relationship.

The show was filmed Monday to Thursday and ended Thursday night about 7:00. After a wrap, "Drinks for the Dogs" began, a time when Doris drummed up business for her pet cause, charging fifty cents per cocktail. The first Thursday night Mr. X came on the scene found the two of them engrossed in conversation on the set bed with Doris not circulating as she usually did. The pair seemed oblivious to the cast and crew who watched, wondering why Doris wasn't anxious to get her makeup off and dash home as always. We thought they were talking about a movie they had made together several years before, but no one guessed Doris and Mr. X were preparing to be an "item."

Doris told me she was interested in Mr. X, despite the fact that he was married and had a family in New York. I cautioned her, "Clara, be careful. Someone is bound to get hurt, and I don't want that someone to be you." "Marzy," she answered, "in a triangle, someone is bound to get hurt." After Doris and Mr. X had made a tentative date, he had not called to reconfirm, so she asked me to call him and find out when they were going out. I was embarrassed to call, but felt this was part of my job. He told me he would like to take her to dinner that evening. What time would be right? They decided on 8:00 PM, a little late for Doris's dinnertime.

I stayed at her home on the first of their several evenings out. Doris acted like a nervous school girl waiting for her date, beautiful in that chamois pant suit and powder blue sweater. She beamed when the doorbell rang; and when she let him in, they kissed romantically. She was hooked. As a rule, Doris told me where she would be, in case I needed to reach her. Not this time. They did not want to go any place people might recognize them because of his family. I don't know when they returned, but the dogs barked, and I was too sleepy to look at the clock.

Between filming different shows, Mr. X had to fly to New York, and Doris missed him. Jacqueline Susann, Doris's east coast spy, knew a mutual friend of the secret boyfriend, and that person kept a close watch on him, a coast-to-coast espionage game. Jackie played her part willingly, vowing as usual to find a man for her friend. She was pleased Doris was finally interested in someone. Mr. X returned to Los Angeles to finish his show contract, and they had more dates. One Sunday morning as I slept at my apartment in Sherman Oaks, the phone rang, with a distraught Alma on the other end. "Mary Anne, where's my daughter? It's 3:00 AM, and she isn't home yet. Where is she?"

Doris did not want her mother to know she was dating a married man so I said, "Alma, I don't know where she is, but she must be all right. Otherwise, you would have heard from her." Alma didn't buy that. "Doris always calls me when she's going to be late. She has done that ever since she was a little girl, and she didn't call this time." I tried to reassure Alma, but that was like telling Niagara Falls not to splash down. She knew I wasn't telling her something. Doris called the next morning to tell me her mother was sitting up in her bed and had greeted her with, "Where have you been? I've been worried sick about you." Fifty years old, Doris was furious at being treated like a school girl who missed her curfew.

At the time of her second TV show with Mr. X, Doris arranged a lunch at her dressing room apartment. She had made sure he had one of the best dressing rooms. Now, with my help she wanted to feed him well. She ordered delicacies for lunch, and I prepared the spread, hoping to be excused when they came in. But Doris insisted I stay. I guess she thought if people knew I was there, no one would suspect an affair. I felt in the way, but kept busy. They embraced for a long time and then ate the lunch I had prepared, the tried-and-true lemon chicken, vegetables, and fruit.

Lemon Chicken

Ingredients: 4 boneless chicken breasts; 1/2 cup butter; 1/3 cup real lemon juice; 1/2 cup flour; 1 tablespoon minced onion; 1 clove minced garlic (optional); 1 teaspoon salt and pepper
Directions:
Pound the chicken breasts. Dredge with flour. Melt the butter in a baking pan. Coat chicken on all sides. Bake at 375, brushing with pan drippings for 30 minutes.
To make the lemon baste, mix the lemon juice, minced onion, garlic, and salt and pepper. Brush the chicken with part of this base, and bake, brushing with the remaining baster for 30 minutes longer or until done. Doris always liked a baked potato and either a crisp lettuce salad or a vegetable. This recipe serves 4.

At the end of the day, Doris was always worn out. After watching the "dailies" she looked forward to heading home. She critiqued each shot in these clips from the day's shooting. That way, if anything had to be re-shot, she knew it immediately. We had another early call the next day. But on the day of the luncheon, Doris seemed to have a surge of energy and was raring to go to Mr. X's after work. I stayed with her while she hurriedly got ready for her date. She sent Del home with the dogs, and mine became the "get-away" car. Doris looked radiant when I dropped her off at his hotel in Burbank. After this, going over there became almost a daily routine as long as they were filming together. Finally he moved into an apartment overlooking Forest Lawn in Burbank, a more secluded and safer location for their dates.

One weekend she wanted me to drive her there. I saved a large poster of him from the show and put it in the trunk, knowing there would be nothing on the walls. Mr. X gave us directions and when we arrived, awaited her with open arms. I sent along a casserole of the chicken she liked, and they had staples for the weekend. It was obvious that both were looking forward to this time together. Doris took in a bag full of things to make the apartment more homey: Kleenex, air spray, and a little figure that had its arms stretched out saying, "I love you this much." Last but not least, she packed her red-and-white flannel nightgown.

They invited me in, but feeling like a fifth wheel again, I declined. Doris had asked me to stay at her home while "she was visiting with her sick friend," and she gave me his private phone number, which his wife did not have. The following weekend I again drove the get-away car. This time Doris packed her bathing suit and books she wanted Mr. X to read. She was sharing the Joel Goldsmith material on spiritual improvement and said they were getting into deep discussions.

Early Saturday morning, I received a frantic call from Doris. "Mary Anne, please come and pick me up right away." I didn't know what had transpired, but I got dressed in a hurry and drove straight to his apartment. A tearful Doris waited—she had been dumped. On the drive back, she cried non-stop. It reminded me of the scene from *Pillow Talk* when Tony Randall drove her away after a mix-up with Rock Hudson. I felt sorry for her.

She stopped long enough to tell me that suddenly Mr. X seemed distant and disinterested. Things had changed in their torrid affair. They were through. Worse—they still had one more show to film. How she dreaded the upcoming week of filming! How was she going to get through it? After all, the script had some romantic scenes, and she told me, "The thought of him turns my stomach." She could have had him written out of the script, but there was no time, and she had to go through with it. This would test her acting ability. She spent the rest of the weekend crying. Doris arrived at the set at her usual 7:00 AM on Monday, the first day of filming for the week, and went straight to make-up in a black mood unlike her usual cheerful disposition. I didn't like this side of her and, thankfully, never saw it again. After each scene she dashed to her dressing room so she didn't have to sit on the set and stare at him. She had been playing a dangerous game and lost.

It strained her to have to work under such conditions, but as a trouper she made it. I guess we both did a little extra praying. As the week progressed, what was normally a joyful atmosphere altered radically. In the hopes of avoiding her former lover, Doris did not mingle with cast and crew as had been her habit. By Thursday she was convinced that Mr. X was interested in someone else on the set, and she was certain she knew exactly who. During the final day of filming, Doris asked me to go to Mr. X's room and get some things back. She handed me a list. I knocked on his door and could hear him ask, "Who's there?" I told him through the closed door. He said that all of Doris's things were in the rented car outside his dressing room. I really didn't care to see him anyway. I gathered the things and noticed that her blender was not all there, but didn't stop to quibble.

While others enjoyed "Drinks for the Doggies," Doris had her own party in her dressing room with her two closest friends on the set, Barbie and Connie. Drinks flowed that night, and no one felt any pain. The more they drank, the more upset she became. I hated to see Doris devastated. Here she was, the top box-office draw in Hollywood, jilted like any ordinary girl. But Doris played with fire in this relationship, and it was bound to explode, with herself the casualty of her own behavior.

I remained at her home over the weekend, and early in the day she continued to tell me how awful Mr. X was. Still, as I walked through the living room, I heard her on the phone with Western Union. She was sending him a wire to "apologize for not acting like a lady the previous week." I couldn't believe what I heard, but if Doris had a change of heart, that was ultimately for the good.

As for "other men" in her life, she has been linked with many. On February 27, 1971, Doris referred to producer Don Genson with admiration. "If you have a brother, that's the way you would like him to be, like Don," she said. Shortly after that she got mad reading all the gossip about her supposed wedding to Don at Terry's hospital bedside. Rumors hit the papers and magazines fast and furiously. Marilyn Beck, a top syndicated gossip columnist of *The Hollywood Exclusive*, ran an "exclusive" on Doris's pending wedding. I called Marilyn on my own, identifying myself as Doris Day's personal secretary, and told her that her "exclusive" was rubbish. I asked her where she got her information, and she replied, "Mary Anne, I got this from very reliable sources at CBS." I began telling her how upset Doris was: there was absolutely no truth to the story at all. After my explanation, Marilyn sheepishly replied, "Well, I guess that makes me look like I have egg on my face."

About the same time, another name, rock super star Sly Stone, became linked romantically with Doris's. Letters poured in from fans all over the world, appalled with her alleged new lover. Oddly enough, Doris didn't know of this one until we got reports from the fans, making no bones about their disappointment over her so-called romance with a black star. Finally Doris decided to call Joyce Haber at the *Los Angeles Times* to go on record, "I only met Sly Stone once, about five years ago at my son's home. There is absolutely no romance between us, but I do admire his musical talent." Apparently the story originated as a publicity stunt to help promote Sly's version of Doris's hit record, "Que Sera, Sera."

Frank Sinatra was another supposed love of her life. Recuperating from her face-lift, Doris asked me to pick up movie magazines. She had not looked at one in years, and they were a revelation. She paged through some, laughing when she got to a story about a romance between her and Ol' Blue Eyes. The story said Frank had offered his Palm Springs home to Doris while Terry recuperated in the hospital. Doris quickly remarked, "My God, I haven't seen Frank since we made *Young at Heart,* and that was in the early 50s."

Doris liked James Cagney, her co-star in *Love Me Or Leave Me,* the movie about the 20s flapper/singer, Ruth Etting. In 1974 "Jimmy," as she called him, invited her to accompany him to an event honoring him with the Lifetime Achievement of the American Film Institute. I happened to have an 8″ x 10″ glossy of them from *Love Me Or Leave Me,* and asked Doris if she would take it with her for him to autograph for me. She agreed. Looking absolutely glowing in a salmon-colored, form-fitting long gown, she went out to meet Cagney as he arrived in a limousine. I never saw him, but the next morning when we had breakfast, she gave me the photo he had autographed. Doris also admired Jimmy Stewart, co-star of *The Man Who Knew Too Much,* who lived nearby in Beverly Hills. We would see him occasionally while bike-riding to Nate 'N Al's, and she stopped to talk to him, introducing me, too.

Late in 1973 a national weekly rag, and other papers and magazines, ran stories like, "Doris finds a new love before millions on TV Show." The front page article read, "When McLean Stevenson of M*A*S*H fame was pinch-hitting for Johnny Carson on 'The Tonight Show,' he walked into a romance with Doris Day, who told the magazine she had difficulties dating because of her superstar status!" Doris promptly wrote to the editor telling him there had never been a romance with Stevenson. She concluded, "Now, regarding my personal quotes in the article, I was supposed to have called myself a superstar? This is utter nonsense, and I have never spoken to the writer or to your paper. Please set the record straight for me. Most Sincerely, Doris Day. PS: Sorry to have to ask you to do this, but I really think we are all being used."

The story behind the story was that Doris hoped "Mac," as she called him, would call her as he had announced to millions of viewers that night on TV. They had been friends for years since he played her boss, Mr. Nicholson, on the second and third season of her show.

Doris and Warren Beatty were at one time supposed to be seeing each other romantically. On one of her rare nights on the town, she attended a party and sat talking with some ladies about work to be done for the animal cause. The women seemed interested in helping, and she wrote her phone number on a piece of paper and gave it to one of them. Beatty, eyeing her all night, sat on one arm of the sofa. He was close enough to memorize her number, she told me, because she did not give it to him, but he still ended up with it.

I lived with Doris at that time, and she wasn't in the house more than five minutes one evening when the phone rang. I knew it wasn't for me, so I turned over and went back to sleep. In the morning she told me the call was Beatty, who confessed he had had a crush on her for some time and took the golden opportunity to memorize her phone number when she gave it to the ladies. Doris told me, "He's too young for me, Marzy, and I really don't want to go out with him. If he calls, and I know he will, please tell him I'm out on my bike, or in the pool, or asleep, just anything."

But he persisted. I got the phone calls for the next few days. Answering his frequent calls, I kept giving excuses as instructed. After a while he must have thought I was not giving her the messages, but she let me handle it. The real story I didn't give him: "Sorry, Mr. Beatty, I did give her all your messages, but the lady you have a crush on doesn't want to go out with you." When Doris told Terry about Warren's calling, he said, "For God's sake, Mother, you don't have to marry the guy! You could have just gone out and had a nice dinner." Not Doris.

Another man who had a crush on her was a Texas oil man, introduced to her by her TV father, Denver Pyle. Denver had known "Tex" from business deals, and he kept bugging Denver to introduce him to Doris. He and a psychic from Georgia, Bob, traveled to Los Angeles periodically on business. Tex showered her with flowers, especially the yellow rose of Texas, and often donated to her animal causes. Doris and I went to dinner a couple of times with them, but she always made it clear she was not in love with him. Tex gave her a 1930 Model A Ford as a friendship token, but she was reluctant to take it although he insisted. Little did I realize at the time that this "non-romance" would impact my future, but that story is for later.

14

A Farewell to Opal

Jacqueline Susann lay in the hospital dying of cancer, and Doris did not want to let on to her friend that she knew about her illness. She gave me a final letter to write and send to her on September 4, 1974. Doris conveyed her sincere love and noted that she would be coming to New York around September 10th and hoped to see Jackie. She would be in town to meet with the Helene Curtis and Studio Girl people for an upcoming Doris Day project with these companies.

She confided to Jackie that she believed her appearance on "The Johnny Carson Show" was a flop. Johnny, she said, had a pinched nerve and was on heavy medication, so he wasn't as sharp as usual. She expressed a desire to be on "The Dick Cavet Show," where real, intelligent talking was the norm.

She told Jackie about her upcoming special for producer George Schlatter and promised her friend that when they came to New York, they could once again ride through Central Park and check on "the baby monkey." But Jackie had become much too ill for that.

On September 10, 1974, Doris and their mutual friend Rack flew to New York. I very much wanted to go with them, but I had to stay behind to care for the home and animals and look after Alma. Then the strangest thing happened. One night with Doris gone, I had a remarkably real dream. I stood in Jackie's hospital room, and she and I had a marvelous visit. Suddenly, the loss I felt by not being able to go dissipated. I had been with her in the dream. When Doris returned I asked her what Jackie's hospital suite looked like. As she described things, I added to them, and she looked at me quizzically. I don't know what happened that night, but I was there in the hospital with Jackie. To this day, I have no explanation, but I had been learning through all the time with Doris that there was more to life than what we can see.

Irving called a couple of days later with sad news—Jackie had died. The next day Doris was again besieged with calls from friends, who knew they were close. To each she relayed some of her thoughts on her friend Opal, better known as Jackie Susann. Doris told them Jackie had informed her about her illness a year earlier, but she didn't want her to feel sorry for her. When Jackie came out to work on her film, *Once Is Not Enough,* she must have been very ill because they would only talk on the phone, and Jackie would apologize for not spending enough time with her friend.

Jackie knew what Doris had gone through with Billy, losing him earlier in the year. I guess she didn't want to bother Doris with her own health concerns. She would say, "I'm just tired, Clara, and I'm working hard on my picture. I haven't a minute to myself." Jackie just told Doris she had to go to the hospital to take care of "the bronchial thing." Doris had been in court, but called Irving constantly, and she was beginning to worry.

"Before I left Los Angeles I was continually talking to Irving," Doris told her friends. "I knew then it was cancer, but he couldn't bring himself to say the word. He just never would say the word to me and he would tell me, 'It doesn't look good, Clara. Pray.'"

I heard her say, "A note and a picture came in the mail to me and it was a picture of Jacqueline and her Joseph. Jacqueline and I went biking in Central Park. She knew I loved to ride a bike, and when we were in New York for those two days, she said, 'Clara, I know a place, and we are going to rent a bike and go through Central Park because I want you to meet the baby monkey, the little chimp, Patty Cake.' Jackie adored all the animals in the zoo. She was an incredible animal person, and that was another one of our many things that we had in common."

Doris told the friends that knowing Jackie was a privilege and their love of animals had bound them together. "Opal, we will grow old together," she had said to Jackie. "We'll just fill the place with animals and we will pick up every stray that we find. Keep working, and I'll keep working. We've got to have enough money to pay for all of this." But they wouldn't grow old together. Doris would go on without one of the best friends she ever had. I received a note from Irving shortly after Jackie's passing.

> *Dear Mary Anne,*
>
> *Thank you for your comforting letter. It is extremely difficult for me to write an adequate response at this time. Rarely has a husband ever been blessed by such expressions of love and respect. Jacqueline Susann was quite a woman. With great affection,*
>
> *Irving Mansfield*

15

The Fans

"All the kooks in town hang out at my house. Actually, all the kooks out of town hang out at my house, too," Doris remarked one morning at Nate 'N Al's. "When I'm out in front, barefoot, and my gardener isn't there, I'm hosing, and they are taking my picture doing that." I was not sure if she was upset because they took photos of her, or because she was in her plain-Jane clothes and hairdo, not being the glamorous movie star.

Doris became annoyed when she wanted to skate in her driveway with rollers in her hair. She came in the door after being outside for about one second, saying, "You can't even roller skate in your own front yard without everyone stopping to take your picture." I could easily identify with those fans.

To solve her dilemma, I suggested she put on a floppy hat to conceal the rollers. She did, and went out for another spin. With her permission I ran to my room for my Super 8 camera and filmed her, skating back and forth. An excellent skater, she did a figure 8, gliding in loops with ease. Little Muffy pranced out to be with her; and while Doris skated, Muffy romped. Doris hammed it up, and we got a big laugh when I showed her the film a few days later. She once commented that she learned to ice skate in *On Moonlight Bay* in one lesson.

If I happened to meet nice, trust-worthy fans, I would tell them to look for her out in front of Nate 'N Al's. After all, I had been richly favored.

I needed to pass it on.

I read most of her fan mail and found that Doris appealed to young and old internationally. Many of the kids aged 15 and younger told her their favorite movies of hers were *Calamity Jane* (1954) and *Pillow Talk* (1959), released before many were born. They became fans from the movie re-runs on TV. In the mid-1970s Doris received a note from the *Family Weekly* with an award for being voted Number One Female Movie Star. She laughed, and after reading the award commented, "I haven't made a film in almost six years." But she still had a big following, and they continued to vote for her.

Doris said she never liked the image of the girl next door that had brought her fame and fortune, but this was the image fans loved. In an interview with BBC on February 3, 1973, the interviewer commented, "During your filming career you were very much labeled with The Girl Next Door tag." She quickly asserted, "I didn't have a thing to do with it. I don't know why I was tagged with that. I still don't know why I was labeled the girl next door. I have people living next door to me, and they don't look like me. Does your next door neighbor look like me?" She laughed. "No, unfortunately, she does not," the reporter conceded.

Following the broadcast she added, "You know what I did want to say and forgot. Maybe you could add it. I have a marvelous Fan Club there in London, and I've dropped all fan clubs because I don't have time to really participate and be active. But that's the one club that I would never give up. They're such marvelous kids, and it's a great group. It is the Doris Day Society, and I wonder if you would say 'hello' to them for me. Would you do that? I love them all."

Doris didn't like it when a TV station featured "Doris Day Week," showing her films for seven days. She did not like watching her old movies, and to my knowledge, she didn't own any of them. I was shocked when I discovered her many awards from years gone by sat locked in closets catching dust, some in a closet in the den where my office was and others relegated to the living room to the "projection area" used when Marty was alive. She seemed in reality to be a totally different person from the girl on film. I found it sad that Doris didn't appear to enjoy her own work, perhaps because she did not have the ego many stars seem to. She confided that she never liked making movies, but added, "Marty had already signed me to do them, and I had to go to work." In particular, she hated *Caprice* and commented that it didn't make any sense—no one could follow that story line. I had to agree with her. I fell asleep the first time I saw it, not like me, the #1 Fan.

Doris selectively answered fan mail. She sent thank-you notes for gifts, but usually told people she wished they had not spent money on her. As I answered these letters and gifts, I was reminded of one such letter I received before we had met. On January 3, 1967, she sent a letter that included the following:

> You girls really shouldn't have done it, and it seems that I say this every year, but I can't stop you. Anyway, since you won't listen to me, I shall graciously accept your lovely gift. It really is a beautiful dish, and the fact that you can make two pieces out of one is terrific. Thank you so much for your thoughtfulness.

Doris said she felt guilty, especially at Christmas and on her birthday, since fans from all over the world would spend their money on valuable gifts. She couldn't keep everything she received, and it became a task to go through all of the pretty wrapped boxes, which might lie around her home unopened for days. Doris appreciated even the smallest, but most of them, even some from dear friends, went to her mother for the Motion Picture Mothers auctions and bazaars. Or, if not, most went to the pet cause, Actors And Others for Animals, for their thrift shop in North Hollywood. Eventually, so many came that Doris asked her friends and fans to please send a donation to their favorite charity in her name instead of gifts.

It began to be impossible to answer all the mail—at least 10 to 20 letters a day at her home and others reaching her via the studios and CBS. She still received mail sent to Warner Brothers, where she had not worked in over 20 years. With postage increasing, she became selective in answering, but those with animal concerns got top priority.

Doris's fans came from all the varied walks of life. I once spent $110 at the Actors and Others for Animals Bazaar in 1973 for lunch for two at the Polo Lounge with Doris just so a "creep" would not win the opportunity. I managed to outbid him, but never arranged to have the lunch. I looked forward to it, but it never came to pass. I was out the $110, but I saved Doris from a strange encounter.

Doris had an unusual ambivalence toward fans. Sometimes she wanted them around and liked to surround herself with people who hung onto her every word. I know, since I was one of those hangers-on. Before I worked for her, she sent Mary, Linda, and me a note following a Saturday breakfast. We took her to the Hideaway Restaurant in the Beverly Wilshire Hotel, and her thank-you note arrived the following Monday. She could sound pretty effusive, but strong appreciation was an authentic part of her personality. She sent her love and praise for "good conversation" and added, "Saturday morning was one of the nicest times I've ever experienced!!! You three are too much and couldn't have been sweeter. Everything was perfect—the food, the place, the daisies, the waiter, and most of all YOU!!!"

For over two years we met happily for breakfast at Nate 'N Al's. Then, one day she decided to call a halt to the weekly meetings. She said, "I think we are all a little old for this." Later we found out that some of the other patrons, people she knew in the industry, may have taunted her for "her girls" clinging to her. This separation lasted for a short time, and then she welcomed us at her booth again. Her mom had been joining us in between times, also, and Alma always seemed to enjoy being with young friends. She added to the breakfasts with her sense of humor.

When Doris answered fans personally, she had a habit of writing, "I would like to meet you one day." I guess she never thought the recipient would really take her up on the invitation. If I had received a letter of encouragement like that when I lived in Indianapolis, I would have been on the next plane. I tried to warn Doris about being so encouraging. She did not fully realize the depth of devotion she inspired.

In 1971, shortly after I began working for Doris, I noticed she called her little Schatzie by a nickname, "Elsie Spray." She'd look at him and call out, "Here comes Elsie Spray." I thought it a rather odd name, but she used it frequently. While looking through the fan mail, I was surprised to see a letter from England from a real Elsie Spray! I ran in to ask Doris about it, and she told me Elsie Spray had been writing for years. Doris would write back and begin by saying, "It would be nice to meet you one day." Now Elsie was about to take her seriously. One afternoon I opened mail and a letter had arrived from Elsie, enclosing what seemed to be a passport photo. I showed it to Doris, commenting, "I think Elsie has a trip to the United States in mind." Doris answered, "Oh, I don't think she'll ever come."

While Doris visited at Kaye Ballard's in Palm Springs for a few days, I was watering the geraniums in the yard on a Friday afternoon when I heard Venice, the housekeeper, call, "Mary Anne, there's a lady here to see you." I could hear the dogs barking and wondered who had come. I didn't encourage friends to drop in at Doris's home. I dashed in to greet the visitor.

There in the vestibule stood a rather plain looking lady. I immediately recognized her from her photo and said, "Elsie, what are you doing here?" She shook from excitement, some of it caused by the pooches leaping at her. I ushered her into the den, just off the vestibule, closing the doors so the dogs could not come in and knock her down. She was very nervous, but after a short time calmed down a bit. She told me she was here for six weeks, and intended to spend that time at Doris's home! She had brought three suitcases and an umbrella into the house. I told her Doris was out of town, but beyond that, she could not stay. She had come to Beverly Hills by cab from the airport, and the cabbie had just dropped her at the address she had indicated. She informed me she didn't have much money, hoping, I suppose I would feel sorry for her and ask her to stay. Doris would be furious, and I needed to get this fan far from Crescent Drive as soon as possible.

What about the YWCA? Located at the old Studio Club in Hollywood, it was safe and cheap. After phoning to ask about rates, I finally convinced Elsie she needed to leave. I put her suitcases in my car, and we drove into Hollywood to get her checked in at the Y. She needed a deposit. Since she had come directly from the plane, she had not had time to exchange pounds into dollars. Fortunately, it was Friday afternoon, and the banks were open. We left her suitcases at the Y, got back into my car, and drove to the nearest bank. I then dropped her off and said I would call on her later in the week. That night Doris called from Palm Springs to check on things, and I told her about Elsie. To my amazement she really didn't seem surprised, but said she was glad I could handle things.

I checked with Elsie once a week, and she was taking in all the sights and visiting studios. Feeling sorry for this disappointed fan, I took her to a restaurant on Sunset Boulevard and to Nate 'N Al's. The last time we went to Nate's, Mary came with us. While there, we saw Steve Lawrence and Eydie Gorme, but Elsie was not interested in them or any other stars. She only wanted Doris.

Elsie continued to say she hoped to meet Doris during her visit. I stayed firm that I couldn't promise anything. Late one evening after we had taken Elsie out, Doris phoned, asking, "Do you think I should see her?" I responded, "Yes, I definitely think you should do that." I knew Elsie would be happy with just meeting her at her gate for a chat and having her picture taken with her. Then Mary got on the phone and described Elsie's body odor. She said to my chagrin, "Clara, I was so embarrassed to be seen with her, and I don't think you should see her." Whether because of that or some other reason, Doris decided not to see Elsie.

A year later I received a note from Elsie's cousin, thanking me for being so nice to her. The letter informed me that Elsie had died. I broke the news to Doris, but she had no comment. Maybe she felt guilty about not taking time to say "Hi" at her fence. The name of Elsie Spray never came up again, and thankfully, Schatzie's nickname was abandoned.

Doris had her share of "nuts," as all celebrities do. The bell at her gate rang day and night. People came to her home whenever the spirit moved them. One weekend I heard the bell ring at 1:00 AM. I rushed to the intercom and asked, "Who's there?" "Is this Doris Day's home?" came the reply. I shot back with, "If you don't leave in two seconds, I'm calling the police. Do you know what time it is?" To my surprise, the person said. "We just arrived from Nebraska and would like to get Miss Day's autograph." I guess they thought Doris should have a card table set up at the California border to give out immediate autographs. It was terribly annoying to have that bell go off at all hours. Doris frequently used to turn the thing off at night, especially during the height of the tourist season. If people were nice and not pushy, I used to ask them to leave their name and address in the mailbox, and Doris would send them a photo. However, if they were pests, I wouldn't hesitate to call the police, who were quick to respond.

Shortly after I began working for Doris, she started receiving weird letters, typed and hand signed with the initial "F." On the 12th of each month, the bell would ring late at night. We would answer, "Who's there?" No reply, never a sound of a car. For several months this continued—the bell late at night, and no one there except for a note in Doris's mailbox from "F." From the tone of the letters, we decided they came either from a deranged man or a lesbian admirer. I voted for a woman, and Doris thought a man. Finally one night, Doris asked me to answer. "Who's there?" I asked. A woman's voice said, "There's a package in the mailbox for Miss Day." Timorously, I waited about half an hour and then walked slowly to the mailbox as Doris watched me from the door. Another present from "F."

My curiosity got the best of me, and, donning my detective hat, I determined to find out who "F" was. Although Doris did not encourage us, Mary and I decided to wait across the street in Mary's car the following month on the 12th. We sat watching in the darkness for hours. Ready to leave, we saw a figure on foot approaching Doris's mailbox. If we heard the dogs barking, we would know "F" had gone toward the gate bell. Sure enough, dog-barking started up, and Mary and I jumped out in the dark and hurried across to discover the identity of the secret and ominous admirer. Mary ran and I walked, as my leg was still not ready for the Olympics, but I caught up with her. Mary asked, "Are you F?" The frightened, mannish-looking woman nervously said, "Yes."

"I knew you would come tonight, and I told Doris you were a woman," I asserted. She grew angry and started mumbling, "Broken my trick, figured it out." Then she ran to her car, which was parked around the corner. I was nervous, not knowing what she would do, but she just took off. Doris soon began receiving even stranger hand-written letters from "F," showing a map of where Mary and I lived and where Doris's mom lived. The writer castigated Doris for sending the "Laurel and Hardy" team after her, furious that she let others read her frighteningly odd letters. After weeks passed, we thought we were rid of her. The next month's 12th came and went without incident.

However, one day I attended an Adoption Day sponsored by Actors and Others for Animals at the kennel where we paid boarding for about seventy dogs. I spotted a person who looked like "F," a volunteer. I had only seen her in the street light, but checked out her license plate so I knew her name. I asked one of the volunteers, and to my surprise, the name given me was the name I had for "F." She had obtained our post office box key. I informed the group at the kennel of her history, insisting she was a threat to Doris. They asked her to leave the organization, and she did so without problems. What a relief to be rid of "F" at last!

Once while living with Doris, she asked me to take friends to the airport, leaving her alone. She was getting ready for a party and did not have time to see them off. When I returned and pulled up to the gates, I saw three police cars and the police patting a man down. He had come numerous times with scripts he wanted Doris to read. This time he began ringing the bell, pulling on the gates, and screaming at her. Within seconds the police arrived with two cars to the front and one down her alley. Fans thought nothing of walking in her flower garden and peering into the windows before the gates were put up after Marty's death and the Manson scare. Even with gates, people climbed over and walked around while the gardeners worked.

One of Doris's pet peeves with fans was interrupting her at a restaurant.

They seemed to wait until the food arrived and then charged over for autographs. She would say, "You sat there fifteen minutes while I was waiting for my breakfast, and you didn't come over until I was ready to eat. Please wait until I'm finished, and I'll be happy to sign an autograph for you." Doris usually acted graciously to fans she met in public or those who caught her in her yard or those she saw while riding her bike through the village.

One Saturday morning Doris, Linda, Mary, and I were having breakfast at Nate 'N Al's. Three girls, obviously fans, sat across from us in a booth, giggling and trying to get up the nerve to come over and talk to Doris. Finally one got bold and walked over and started giving Doris a sad tale about her dog who had just died. She went on with the story, which got worse, until Doris dissolved in tears. I tried to stop the girl, but she kept on, with Doris attentive to every word. Then the other girls came over and introduced themselves. Doris chatted and began telling them about her animal group. After about fifteen minutes they left, and I went to the ladies' room. While in the stall I heard people come in, giggling and talking about giving Doris the wild dog sympathy story I had just heard. They left before I could say anything, but I returned to our booth and told Doris what I had overheard—the story was fake. She was still teary-eyed, and I was angry. How could anyone pull such a stunt? Doris wore her heart on her sleeve, and an animal cruelty story got to her more than any other ploy.

I don't know if sometimes Doris was a poor judge of character or if the people she met in the streets were great actors, but often she'd come home and tell me about some "fantastic lady who really loves animals and wants to help in our animal group." She would ask me to call the supposed animal lover, and I'd discover that person was not at all interested in our group, much less working for animal causes. People would jump at anything to talk to her.

Doris's mom loved to answer the door, but never got used to using the intercom to the gate. She always called out from the door, "Who's there?" Alma frequently wanted to make sure people knew she was Doris Day's mother. Often they took her for the cook, which didn't please her. She was very good with the fans and liked to set up plans for admirers to meet Doris. A boy from Florida came daily with a bouquet of daisies in the hope of seeing her, and Alma kept encouraging him to "come tomorrow. I'll be sure to fix it so you can see Doris." Tomorrow never came. Doris was not happy when her mother would plan fan-meeting sessions and most often sent regrets. As years went along, the immediacy we early fans had experienced by necessity had to close down. Times changed in the 70s when I was there.

Some people got lucky, met her, and chatted, but others never had that opportunity. A young Navy man had been writing Doris one or two letters daily, all the same, saying he was lonely and in love with her. He was too nervous to introduce himself at the first Actors and Others for Animals bazaar in 1971, but managed to get up the courage to tell her about his next trip home the following year. Doris agreed to meet at Nate 'N Al's. You could sense the thrill this gave him.

Three Chicago girls wrote Doris for a couple of years, and when they arrived in Los Angeles one summer, they got in touch with her. I was in Chicago. When I returned, Doris told me all about all the activities she and the girls from the Windy City did together. As I left her home on a Friday night, she told me, "I've done more with those girls than any other movie person would do, and I know they're leaving on Monday, and I'm not going to call them. I've had it with them, and I've seen them enough." So I was surprised the next day when I saw her with them at Nate 'N Al's. Doris's maid Lilly called to say, "You'll never guess who's over here swimming!" Sure enough, the Chicago girls were splashing in the pool. I wonder what made Doris change her mind?

Doris was one of the few stars who actively participated in a fan club of her own. In 1973, shortly after her London trip, the two heads of her club —Sheila Smith from London, the person whom I had originally contacted many years ago, and Valerie—flew to the States to attend the International Fan Club Convention in St. Louis. They came away with first prize for maintaining an outstanding club. Their next stop was Los Angeles, where Doris was delighted to see them again, having just had a visit with many members in London two weeks previously.

She determined to show them a good time, wining and dining them at Musso Frank's on Hollywood Boulevard, the oldest restaurant in Hollywood. They attended a charity fashion show and luncheon at the Century Plaza Hotel, where Doris and Biggest strolled down the aisle to a standing ovation. Also during their stay they helped man Doris Day's Dog House booth at the 34th annual Motion Pictures Mothers, Inc., with Alma and Doris. She appreciated all the work they had done for her over the years. After a week of partying with Doris, the two flew home. When they landed, a bouquet of flowers with a huge fruit basket arrived there for them with a card reading, "With love from Doris, Alma, Mary Anne, Mary and Linda. Welcome Home."

One day Doris received a sweet letter from an elderly lady in northern California. She sent a photo of herself looking cute in her "Doris Day" out-fit, a dress she had purchased from Joseph Magnin, one of the nicest depart-ment stores in southern California, where Connie Edney bought most of the wardrobe Doris wore on her series. Doris wrote back to her saying she would love to meet the lady and sending her answering-service phone number. Naturally, the lady made the trip to Los Angeles within a few months and gave us a call. Doris was out, and I took the message. When she returned, I told her the lady with the Doris Day dress was in town and would like to meet her. She gave me some excuse as to why she could not. "Be sure and tell her that on her next trip we'll meet." I phoned and asked the woman to call next time she was in town. A couple of months later she did, and Doris again was a no-show. The woman never called back. I felt sorry because Doris had gotten her hopes up by giving her a phone number.

Doris could be extremely kind to some fans, but how she decided who to befriend was beyond me. At least she seemed to try. As I have mentioned, three Australian girls met her for the first time in 1967—in fact, at the bak-ery the day I met her. Over the years, Doris went out of her way to make the Aussies feel welcome both in Beverly Hills and later in Carmel on their many trips. I know it meant a lot to them to have this special bond.

On one of the Aussie girls' visits to the States, Mary and I entertained them at dinner in our apartment in Sherman Oaks. Doris's mom lived next door, and we invited Doris, Alma, and the three girls for dinner. One of them, Joan Barr, an excellent seamstress, knew of Doris's love of hats. She made about a dozen cute hats for Doris, some like caps and others big and floppy, and Doris tried them on and paraded around showing them off to us. We were young fans trying to process the fact that Doris Day was visitng our home, enjoying the attention. Her mom had a good time, too. In those early days of my time in Hollywood, we were all excited beyond words by celebrity. Later for me, at least, as fanhood went through several phases and turned into friendship, many deeper values evolved as I came to know my boss.

It sometimes makes me wonder what being a fan is about. In the case of Doris Day, some sort of idealization of the best in woman-kind has to be involved. And let's face it—outstanding physical beauty draws people. But in the case of Doris, fans were and are attracted to beauty that is not just skin-deep but expresses qualities of sincerity, joy, and fun. There have to be other kinds of subconscious motives for immersing oneself in fanhood—wanting to identify with someone who is very successful, and joining with others who have similar interests—the "clubbing" instinct. Sometimes, as in the case of "F," fanhood declines into something odd and even dangerous. Perhaps being a fan differs from decade to decade, too. Some of the "stars" today exhibit bizarre or undesirable behavior. Perhaps people have always been fascinated by strange or dippy stars, but Doris Day does not fit that category. Her history has shown her a perennial favorite, usually for the best of reasons.

One big Doris Day fan, a handyman named Bob, had a brilliant idea. He asked me if she would be using her tickets to the Academy Awards. Bob thought that if Doris wasn't going to attend, he and his wife and a friend and I could go. I said I did not know but would find out. To my knowledge Doris had not been to an Academy Awards show in years. I found she was happy to make arrangements for the four of us to go in her place. Bob and his wife donned their best clothes, and I asked David, a mutual friend of Doris's and mine to be my date. None of us had ever dreamed we would be going to the Academy Awards.

April 2, 1974, David picked me up to attend the 47th Annual Academy Awards held at the Dorothy Chandler Pavilion. We met Bob and his wife at the theater. The color of your ticket designated what walkway you would use to enter. Stars were everywhere, and so were the paparazzi, all very exciting. Since we had "star" tickets, we were asked to use a designated VIP aisle, the coveted red-carpet area. Walking in front of us were Paul Newman and Joanne Woodward and, behind us, Billy DeWilliams and his wife, and also Paul and Linda McCartney. As we paraded down the red carpet, we saw the press standing behind the ropes, including two of the most popular Hollywood gossip columnists, Rona Barrett and Army Archerd. No press pass, fake or real, ever got me this "in" before. Flash bulbs popped everywhere. After finally threading our way through, we got into an elevator with Walter Matthau and Shirley MacLaine. I could hardly believe this was happening to the little girl from St. Agnes Academy in Indianapolis!

David Niven served as master of ceremonies. One way I can remember this particular Awards presentation is that it was the year of the streaker! Right before all eyes, a man named Bob Opel crashed the show without a stitch on. Niven, a little shocked, commented on the man's "short-comings," and Elizabeth Taylor, who was next, said, "What an act to follow."

After the ceremony, we gathered at the Beverly Hilton for an impressive dinner with stars shining everywhere. I was grateful to Bob, who had the idea of asking about Doris's tickets. The next day she wanted to know about the party, and I shared my observations and thanked her for the opportunity to attend one of America's most important entertainment events.

One summer when I lived in the household, a woman called on Doris's answering-service line. She had somehow obtained the number from CBS, and told me about a girl in the east who adored Doris. This kid was a great animal lover and groomed pets, according to the woman, and all she wanted was to say "Hi" to Doris. I explained that Doris did not make a habit of talking to fans on the phone, but I would ask her and go from there. Surprisingly, she said she would like to talk to the girl, and I made arrangements for the call.

Two weeks later, we placed the call, and Doris talked for over fifteen minutes. I stayed on the other phone while she spoke on the phone from her bedroom. The conclusion went something like this:

Girl: I'd like to meet you one day if I'm ever in California.
Doris: Of course.
Girl: You know you're welcome here too anytime.
Doris: That's really nice, and I'll look forward to meeting you. I'll be in touch with you, and I'll write you very soon.
Girl: Oh, fantastic!
Doris: And you hang in there and keep up the good work and give a kiss to all your babies. OK, darling. Bye, honey.

During the conversation, Doris gave the girl her address and took down the girl's address so she could keep in touch, because the young woman was doing impressive work in her community. Doris commented that she wished the girl lived in California so that she could help with our animal cause.

A few weeks passed, and I received a call from the lady who called me in the first place concerning the young lady. Her conversation was most interesting and probably a demonstration of the ambivalence with which Doris viewed fans.

Lady: I called because of you. You were the kind, gorgeous lady that got us the phone call and as a consequence her address, and my friend has written to her. You were instrumental in all of this.

MA: I was happy to do it for you.

Lady: I just want you to know you are so fantastic, and I wanted you to know that I was thinking of you. Believe it or not, I have you on my mind. You were good to me and did me a favor.

MA: I've been a fan myself, so I know what it means to get through to her.

Lady: But you know a strange thing, and I'm saying this off-the-record. The young girl wanted to go to California and donate her services to your organization and do charity work. She really wanted to do this, and I said, "Go ahead, that's up to you, entirely." She wrote to Doris about doing that and never received any answer. I was really surprised that she never heard from Doris. I'm not a fool. I feel that a personality does not have to answer you, and she has every right not to. She's been very nice, Doris Day, and owes my friend nothing. I feel she just doesn't want to be bothered.

MA: It seems unfortunate that after talking to the girl and really encouraging her, Doris didn't follow through.

Was I surprised that Doris never answered the girl? Doris was usually kind to fans. In all fairness, how can any one star deal face-to-face with thousands of admirers? It's probable these moments of over-encouraging just came out of Doris's good intentions.

16

Moving Out
of the Crescent Drive House

Doris believed that "what you are seeking is seeking you." We looked for a housekeeper for many months, with no viable prospects. When talking with agencies, I stressed that any applicant must appreciate canines. A significant pause came after I answered their question, "How many dogs do you have?" Somehow the number 11 eliminated everyone on the agencies' lists. We finally gave up after many attempts to find help through employment services.

One day in November, 1973, a friend sent a housekeeper in need of a job. After Doris interviewed her, she decided this woman was the right one. She was a black lady named Lilly, who looked like Hattie McDaniel from *Gone With The Wind*. And she loved dogs.

After a few weeks on the job, Doris was pleased with Lilly and loved the interest she took in the doggies. At last I made my reservations to go home for Christmas. I mentioned to Doris that now that she had Lilly, I was thinking about moving back to my own apartment, but Doris asked me to stay.

I had a wonderful visit with my mother and friends. Everyone wanted to know what it was like to live with a movie star. I shared a little with them and told them this was all a dream come true, but, beyond that, she had become a sincere friend. They looked in wonderment, everybody so happy that I finally was doing what I had set out to do years before.

After a 10-day visit with my mother, I flew to Los Angeles, and Doris waited for me the night I arrived at her home. She wore her long, pink satin lounging robe, with the lights dim, as usual. We sat in the living room, and she said, "Mary Anne, I think we have to have a little talk." I said, "Sure, Clara, what do you want to talk about?" A dozen things ran through my mind and from the tone of her voice, I knew whatever she had to say was serious, and we both seemed a little nervous. Hesitantly, with a drink in hand, she said, "Marzy, we are going to have to go back to our old way of living. Nana is moving back in because her doctor said her eyes are bad, and she shouldn't be driving over Coldwater Canyon anymore. It's too dangerous with her eyesight."

This did not surprise or dismay me at all, because I knew Doris's home was not my permanent residence. Besides, I was a little anxious to get back into the real world. As much as I enjoyed living with Doris and was pleased she wanted me, it was a temporary arrangement. I had been glad to help in her time of need when Nada disappeared, but I felt like a cloistered nun, with my social life limited and my work only a labor of love because the salary was modest.

Doris went on, "I've depended too much on you, Mary Anne, and that's not healthy for either of us. It will be much better this way." Then she hugged me. I had hardly expected to hear these words before I had even a chance to take my coat off. Probably Doris had wondered all day how to break the news to me. She seemed relieved once she spoke her mind, and we understood the change was best for both of us.

Some people thought I would be upset. They knew how much I enjoyed living with Doris, and I guess they thought I would fall apart if I had to move. Ruth called the next day to see if I was OK. She had a dream the night before that I had committed suicide! Doris came to rely on me, but I was not bound to her in my own life. I would continue to serve as secretary for as long as it worked out for us.

Doris did not expect me to move right away, but Mary and I began looking for an apartment. With "The Doris Day Show" long over, I had no need to live in the Valley anymore. We found a perfect apartment on the outskirts of Beverly Hills on Clark Drive, just one mile from Doris's. It was just right because I never knew when she might need me, day or night. Doris was happy we didn't move too far away.

Once I moved, Alma settled into the front bedroom, where I had been the past year. Then things began to change in the household, as they often do when parents live with children. Doris seemed uptight. She had said, "I could never live with my mother," and her friends were shocked when they heard the news. The two of them had kept their distance and gotten along, but now they had to face day-to-day living under one roof.

Alma was social, used to being around people, the life of the party. Doris, on the other hand, was almost a loner and glad to have her home as a retreat from the maddening crowds that had surrounded her for years. Her life and attitude, and her mother's, were worlds apart, and all this added to the challenge. As Alma aged, she wanted Doris's undivided attention more than ever and Doris wasn't able to give that. She had a life of her own. Lilly helped to keep things on an even keel. She would often sing gospel tunes as she worked. When she was a teenager, she had sung back-up with Mahalia Jackson, and her voice seemed to have a similar ringing, resonant confidence. Lilly and I became friends, enjoying one another's company. I encouraged her to sing professionally again. On many weekends I would take her out to brunch for a change of scenery, since her family lived back in Chicago.

When I was living with Doris, she was carefree, full of life, not at all moody. She seemed to enjoy her independence and privacy. Even though we were not living under ideal circumstances, without a housekeeper, Doris and I made the most of our situation, and she appeared content, but she was not herself after her mother moved in.

On February 7, 1974, Alma and Doris traveled out of town to attend Terry's wedding to Melissa Whittaker, a beautiful woman with long, dark hair. She had a young daughter and had known Terry a few years. I had hoped to attend the wedding. Both Doris and Terry had invited me, but at the last minute, Doris asked that I return from my apartment to the house to stay with Lilly to watch the dogs and to manage household affairs. I was disappointed because I had bought a new outfit for this special wedding. I didn't go, but sent my camera with Doris, who assured me she would have someone take pictures. She returned with my camera full. Doris and Alma were so happy for Terry. I heard later that Terry seemed surprised that I was not there.

As Alma demanded more attention under Doris's nose, Doris began telling Lilly and me, "I've got to get my mother out of the house and into her own apartment. It's driving me nuts." Alma was an aging stage mom. When Doris was an up-and-coming star, her mother did practically everything for her, including raising Terry while Doris was singing on the road with the band, answering fan mail by the bags full, and doing whatever was needed. She basked in the limelight.

Later, as Doris achieved superstardom, she wasn't going to depend on her mother anymore. She could pay to have help. To Doris's credit, she wanted to give her mom the opportunity to share in some of her success, including her in many activities. Unfortunately, I don't think Alma saw it that way; she saw her responsibilities and importance eroding. I was one of several people doing what she had formerly done, and she often focused on me.

Doris tried to keep Alma busy. She even had her do the grocery shopping. She asked Lilly to make a list and leave it by the phone, and Alma would shop several times a week. Much of the food purchased was for feeding the dogs, for whom Lilly would prepare a chicken stew of three boiled chickens, cut up, mixed with grated carrots and long grain brown rice. In 1974 A. E. Hotchner, the author of her biography from William Morrow, came to work with Doris. That first day he smelled the aroma of this fabulous chicken creation permeating her home. Doris showed "Hotch" around, and when they came into the kitchen, he saw the roaster bubbling. He said, "This reminds me of when my mother used to cook stew for us." Lilly winked and replied, "This is the dog's dinner tonight." We had a big laugh.

Jackie Susann had arranged for the Morrow book project. She believed Hotchner would be the perfect writer to work with Doris, and she was right. He wrote the 305-page book after he interviewed Doris for five months that year. They went back to her guesthouse for three to four hours at a time. Usually, she was drained by the time the sessions ended, and he must have covered topics that made her search her past and her heart. Sometimes she came back to the kitchen in tears, but all in all, she said she felt good about the book. Doris was proud of her story despite the tragedies she'd had. "I'm a survivor," she said. "I have a round bottom, and I bounce back. I don't regret anything. I'm very happy now living the nicest life I can live, and if I can get that in the book, I guess I'll give people hope."

Doris had mentioned to Jackie that she had been asked to be spokeswoman for Studio Girl Cosmetics, a division of Helene Curtis. After numerous months of consultation, the deal was finalized. Many reporters wanted an interview, especially the ones from Chicago, Studio Girl headquarters. A woman writer for the *Chicago Daily News* spent four hours chatting with Doris in her den, and I sat in on this session. Following the interview, Doris remarked that the reporter was a nice person, but very impressed with herself and her clothes. The woman had boasted to her, "I have on an Yves Saint Laurent denim outfit. It cost about $700."

To that remark Doris proudly announced, "I'm in my Sears catalog $8.88 denim jeans and my $4.99 shoes, also from Sears!" The reporter almost fell off her chair, surprised that Doris Day, the clothes horse of the silver screen, would be attired that way and admit it. Before the woman left, she asked for some candid photos of Doris so she could run them with her story. Doris volunteered me to take and send whatever she needed. I took some black-and-white photos of her with Biggest in the backyard, which later ran in the paper with the interview, but I never received photo credit.

Increasingly, Alma seemed jealous over my role as secretary. Doris begged us to put up with her mother, knowing she could be difficult. I felt sorry for Doris, but I also understood Alma's position. She felt slighted because I was paid to do what she used to. I had been warned by many on the TV set and by friends of Doris that if I got too close to Doris, I would be on Alma's you-know-what list. I wish she had realized that we both loved the same lady, and all I wanted was what was best for her daughter and her, too.

Tension grew between the two after I left. As the weeks went by, they plagued each other with increasing annoyances. Doris encouraged her mother to take trips and to visit friends, in the hopes a change in scenery would help. She would tell Lilly and me she wanted to get her mother into her own apartment. It would be best for all. I must say Lilly and I agreed with her since Doris was stretched tight as a drum—not the woman I had lived with the past year.

Doris's birthday on April 3, 1974: When I entered her bedroom, ready to wish her "Happy Birthday," I found her in tears in the middle of her bed. "Clara, what on earth is wrong? It's your birthday. You should be happy." She kept crying and mumbled, "My mother hates me. My mother hates me." Alma was out of town for a couple of weeks, and she hadn't heard from her. It was noon in Houston, and no birthday message had come from Alma. Despite the fact that Doris used to say that birthdays "didn't mean much," they did to her at this time. I didn't let on what I knew, but a surprise was about to happen, and things would soon look brighter.

A couple of weeks before, Terry had asked me to help throw a surprise birthday party for his mom at the new Hungry Tiger Restaurant in Westwood, aiding him with the guest list. Together we went down a list of names, and when I asked, "What about Ruth and her husband?" Terry promptly said, "No, they are my grandmother's friends." He understood the present situation in his mom's home. About 25 people came to her party, and Doris was gratified with this celebration, especially since it was Terry's idea. With tears of joy and surrounded by people who loved her, Doris beamed like a child. Alma, of course, loved her daughter and called that night. She had been busy with her family, and time had slipped away.

Frequently Doris would take weekend trips with Rack or Kaye Ballard. In Las Vegas she saw Charlie Rich, one of her favorite singers, and came home happy with the news that "Charlie dedicated his song, 'The Most Beautiful Girl in the World' to me three times." She played his records and tapes constantly and often danced to them in her room. Sometimes in late 1974 she seemed like the "old" Doris I knew, the happy one.

Another weekend she asked me to stay at the house with her mother and Lilly to take care of things. Her parting words: "Whatever you do, if you should go out, please do not leave my mother alone with the dogs." We just took Alma with us if we had to leave the house, and things worked out satisfactorily. One day with Doris away, Alma came into the kitchen where I was fixing breakfast, and said, "It's because of me that you got your job. I fought for you girls so that Doris would like you, and you have me to thank for your job." I knew that—she was a big help in the beginning when we first saw Doris at the bakery. I will always be grateful to Alma for pulling for us. Denver Pyle phoned at my apartment about a year after I was working with Doris and told me, "Mary Anne, you must be really good because Doris doesn't keep anyone so long as you've been there." I thanked him, saying, "I'm just doing what Doris wants me to do. I'm pleased that she likes me and my work."

Now that I was out of the house, I took a two-week summer vacation to see relatives in Chicago and Indianapolis. When I returned, Doris told me of our "new secretarial " routine. Terry wanted me to help him in his new office with Equinox Records in the RCA Building in Hollywood. But Doris quickly informed me she wanted me to be with her, also. So I would be with her in the mornings and then go to Terry's in the afternoon. Happy with that arrangement, I looked forward to learning the record business. During this time I signed up for an evening course at UCLA on "How to Get a Song Published and Get a Record Deal," and looked forward to each session in the hope of helping Lilly with her gospel music.

Terry's partner was Bruce Johnston of Beach Boy fame. Their first hit had been "Hey, Little Cobra" in 1964 by the Rip Chords (the name they used to record their early hits). Terry sang the lead, and Bruce the high harmony. That song has always been a favorite of mine. Terry, recovered and clean, had a wonderful sense of humor and was great to work with. I liked being at the studio and watching the birth of a record. With everyone stimulating and interesting and eager to get things done, we all had great rapport.

My new schedule continued until the day Alma left for Houston to again visit her family. Doris and I drove her to the airport early in the morning and came back to Doris's home after having breakfast at Nate 'N Al's. About noon I was getting my papers together in my attaché case and was just about to walk out when Doris saw me. To my surprise she said, "Mary Anne, I don't want you to go to Terry's anymore. I need you here from now on." I had to assume that Terry and Doris had discussed this, but later in the afternoon Terry called, "Mare, where are you? Aren't you coming to the office? I need you." I reported his mother's instructions. He had no clue about the new schedule, but since she was paying me, I stayed with her.

During much of 1974 Doris met with her lawyers. The innocence she portrayed on the screen and which was true of her in real life proved a financial trap, as I've mentioned earlier. She had trusted the family finances to Marty, and he, in turn, entrusted their blooming empire to longtime business associate and legal advisor, Jerome Rosenthal, whose clients included Ross Hunter, Van Johnson, Gordon MacRae, and Ava Gardner. After Marty's death in 1968, Terry, then 32, met with Rosenthal to discuss his mother's estate, only to find that for the previous two decades she had been defrauded.

Months passed, with the situation not easy to straighten out. One afternoon Terry came to the house and told his mother she might have to sell her home to pay off Marty's debts. She was dismayed. "I trusted my husband," was all she could say. At Terry's urging, Doris went to court. After 13 suits over six years, an ecstatic Doris Day, whose theme song had been "Que Sera, Sera," found another happy ending—this time scripted by Los Angeles Superior Court Judge Lester Olson. On September 18, 1974, the headline of the *Los Angeles Times* proclaimed, "Doris Day Wins $22 Million." Although I wasn't in court with her on that day, I came to the celebration lunch at Yamato, a popular restaurant with superb Oriental cuisine in Century City.

Doris was aglow, this long ordeal finally over. All the meetings she had with her attorneys had paid off. Doris said, "It's been my own little Watergate, and I'm glad it's over." But her legal battles did not daunt her positive spirit. She often said, "I never lose faith. Sometimes, when things are blackest, nice things happen."

Tribute to Terry

Doris Day's son, Terry Melcher, was a gentle man who did many things for his mother—everything from handling her finances to making sure all her movies were released, her complete music album available on CD, and the five seasons of "The Doris Day Show" copied on DVD. He appreciated my working for her—even more, my caring about her, realizing she needed a friend's help with the many responsibilities of her career plus her second one, animal protection.

When I knew him, Terry was active in the music world. He used to come to his mom's home with his friend and partner in the music business, Bruce Johnston of the Beach Boys. I enjoyed listening to the two standing by Doris's piano singing "I Write The Songs." They sang it repeatedly. Barry Manilow had a big hit with that song, but it was Bruce's creation. Alma hoped Doris and Terry would record an album together as Frank and Nancy Sinatra had done, but that never came to pass.

However, one evening in 1974 Terry, Bruce Johnston, and Tony Martin, Jr., were working on Terry's first LP album called, "Terry Melcher" on the Equinox label. Terry wanted Doris to sing harmony with him, but she resisted. After a little coaxing, she agreed to go to the studio one night. I went, too. At first Terry, Bruce, and Tony, along with Spanky McFarlane, recorded some songs in the booth, as Terry, ever the perfectionist, adjusted controls and reached for better performances. Finally, Doris put on the headphones and walked into the booth. She soon showed enjoyment and asked the sound technician to put her voice up a little louder. Terry was pleased his mother would record with him.

Terry died too young of melanoma at the age of 62 in November, 2004, leaving behind his wife Terese and son Ryan—and a mother who grieved for him, but loved the life he had given to the world and to her.

With the mother-daughter conflict unresolved, Alma left after the court case and stayed away for a month. Doris kept telling me, "As soon as Nana gets back from Houston, she's going to have to move and find an apartment." She meant business this time.

Doris was asked to speak at the "Blessing of the Animals" at All Saints Episcopal Church in Beverly Hills on St. Francis Day, October 5, 1974. Her appearance was purposely not announced so that only those truly interested in animals would attend. She enjoyed seeing the children with their pets, even a pair of ducks called "Nate" and "Al." She later commented to Linda and me at the original Nate 'N Al's, "I went over, and all the children were there with their dogs and cats, little ducks, kittens and puppies. I stood up and told them, 'If you don't take care of them, you're going to have me ringing your door bell.'"

With Alma still in Houston, Doris asked me to spend the weekends of October 5th and the 12th at her house. Lilly left early on Sunday, returning late Monday, and Doris didn't want to be alone, especially at night. I had nothing planned those weekends and gladly stayed with her.

Doris looked forward on Sundays to spending time with her dogs and lying by the pool. So much of her time had been spent rehearsing for a CBS Special co-starring John Denver for 1975. We still had to be careful to keep the dogs separated, and that day I came up with the idea of taking Biggest for a Sunday ride, which left her to herself with no worries. Biggest and I drove up Pacific Coast Highway to Malibu, and I took him past his mother's old beach house. He didn't even take a second look. We came back on Sunset Boulevard to the beautiful park across from the Beverly Hills Hotel up the street from Doris. We stayed out until 5:00 PM, giving her the afternoon to enjoy her home without interruptions. When we returned, she was knee deep in dog food: feeding time. It had done her good to have the time for herself. She laughed when I told her I took Biggest to Malibu.

The next day the doorbell began ringing insistently, with Rona Barrett at the door, frantically looking for her lost dog Lord. Did Doris know of any dog in heat on her block? We immediately started making phone calls. Rona was a worrying wreck, and Doris sympathized. We kept trying to locate the dog, but were short on leads.

It had been fun dividing my time between Doris and Terry, but with Doris active in TV work again, I was at her beck and call. As she was going to rehearsal each day, I was kept busy doing more housework than secretarial work, and not too pleased being more part-time domestic than "super sec." Alma made her grand return on October 15th. Doris and I were to meet her at the airport, but last-minute rehearsal plans for her special changed, and she asked me to go alone. Alma told me about the visit she had with her family and seemed happy to be back. The next day I went about my business as usual. Well after the noon hour, Alma came into my office and asked, "Mary Anne, aren't you going to Terry's office this afternoon?" I mentioned that Doris changed my schedule and that from now on, I was to remain at home with "the boss." Alma was unhappy hearing that, and she left the office. She was not pleased with Doris's new schedule either, which kept her away so much. Doris seemed eager to get out of the house and go to rehearsal, with Lilly and me at home with Alma. Perhaps Alma sensed that.

Still no news about Rona's dog, and that upset Doris further. We tried everything, but the dog had disappeared into thin air. She called Rona each night, hoping for good news. When I stopped by Doris's home on Saturday, October 19th, she was crying into the phone. Lilly said she had received news that Rona's dog was found dead in the bushes by the actress's home. Doris was weeping hysterically over a dog she had never met.

When her tears subsided, I asked if she planned to attend the cocktail party fund raiser the next day for Cat Care, a local cat charity. She never committed herself to anything like a personal appearance for an animal group. Besides, she was too upset about Rona's dog to think about a party. She and her mother were to go to dinner with Tex the oil man that night, and she was trying to get presentable. Tex, the long time fan Denver Pyle introduced to Doris two years before, was in town on business. Her relationship with him remained merely platonic from what I could see. A nice man, about six feet tall, balding and a little chunky, he did not seem Doris's type. He gladly helped support the animal cause, and that may have been why she paid attention to him.

I called Tex to say "Hi" and tell him I would see him on his next trip to LA. We had mutual friends and got together whenever he was in town. He was taking Doris and Alma to dinner, and after that he would catch the midnight flight back to his ranch. He sounded very happy about his "dates." In a little over 48 hours, things would change significantly for everyone.

Alma Day and Terry Melcher on Terry's wedding day in 1974.

Doris and Big-gest, photo taken by Mary Anne for Chicago Daily News *story in October, 1974.*

Doris's backyard in Beverly Hills. That's the chaise I dove after to get it out of the pool.

Doris at my apartment (top and bottom) tried on hats made by an Australian fan in 1974.

Buffy and Doris posed together at my place when they came for dinner in 1974.

Here I am with "Doc" Anderson and Denver Pyle in 1974. Doc was a psychic.

17

The Party's Over

To get the chronology exact, on Thursday, October 17, 1974, Tex had come to town on business. Over time we had commented to each other on Tex's drinking problem; however, no one knew how bad it was. After going to dinner with Doris and her mom on Saturday, October 19th, he had returned to his hotel room to meet with friends of ours in Actors and Others, who were going to drive him to the airport.

Since this happened to be the weekend of the Cat Care fund raiser, I had responsibilities for that event. I arrived early at the Cat Care site Sunday afternoon, October 20th, to help with the guests and to set things up. No one knew if Doris would show, but since it was at a home down the block, I felt almost sure she would come. The party started at 2:00 PM and moved into high gear as I kept an eye on the front door. At about 4:00 PM Alma and Tex walked in hand in hand, looking like they had already started to party. Tex came over to me and said, "Get Alma a chair, and don't give her anything to drink." Alma grabbed on to me and said, "Don't give him anything to drink. He's had enough, and make sure he sits down." This was not good.

Just then the door opened, and in came Doris and Rack arm in arm, neither registering what was going on with Alma and Tex. Soon, Doris came over and whispered, "Don't give Tex anything to drink, Mary Anne." With that she started to circulate, staying at the other side of the room and leaving

Tex near me on a couch. I was surprised to see him at the party since he was booked already on the midnight flight. I told myself that his drinking problem, often observed by us, was playing into this situation.

Tex stayed put on the sofa, while Doris kept her distance. Suddenly, as he rose to head across the room, his signature boot caught on the bear claw leg of the huge coffee table, and he crashed to the floor. We weren't sure if he had collapsed or just tripped over the table leg, but very embarrassed, he couldn't get up. Doris and I were the first at his side, but needed help to get him into a car and back to his hotel. She asked Moury and his wife Sandy, friends from Actors and Others, to drive him. They were the couple supposed to have driven him to the airport the previous night. Doris asked me to go along and let her know how he was after the hotel doctor had checked him out.

The four of us arrived at the hotel and, with the support of bellmen, got Tex to his room. The phone was ringing when we arrived, and he asked me to answer. I picked it up and heard a woman's voice and quickly handed the phone to Moury. It was Mrs. Tex. She had been waiting for him to return home Saturday as he originally planned and was furious he had remained in Los Angeles. Tex had said he was in the process of getting a divorce, but this all sounded quite complicated, forecasting trouble. The house doctor arrived within minutes and indicated Tex might have had a slight stroke. He asked about medications and after examining Tex, stated that he was on some significant prescription drugs. He told us Tex had diabetes, a fact new to everyone in the room. The doctor said Tex could fly home one day late after all, if someone went with him. I called Doris with the update and she asked to talk to Tex. Meanwhile Moury on another phone made reservations for the two of them to return to Texas on the 9:30 PM flight, per Mrs. Tex's orders.

Tex continued talking to Doris, and when he hung up, he announced to our amazement that she wanted him to come to her home. Moury agreed to drive him and left his luggage in the hotel to be picked up on the way to the airport. While Moury went to get the car, I slipped into a phone booth to verify the story. Rack answered Doris's phone, and I asked her if she really wanted Tex to come. She repeated the question to Doris in the background feeding the dogs. I could hear her say, "Tell Mary Anne to bring him over. He begged to come over."

I didn't know what was going on; Doris's part in this wasn't clear now. Was Doris making some sort of claim on him? His irritated wife was waiting back home. But as of now we needed to get this confused, ill, and inebriated oil man to "the boss's" house. We drove over and helped Tex into the living room, where he flopped onto the sofa. Moury gave the report from the doctor and told everyone he was flying Tex home on Mrs. Tex's orders. Rack began questioning me about what the doctor had said and then announced she intended to call her personal doctor in on the case.

Everything happened so quickly. Moury figured he better clue Rack in on what the doctor had told him about the pills, booze, and Tex's diabetes. That struck a nerve with her as it had with us. We had just heard that he was diabetic when the hotel doctor examined him. He was not at all in good health—not surprising, given his lifestyle of eating at fancy restaurants and drinking too much and who knew what else. I begged Rack to convince Doris to let him get on that plane. The man's wife was demanding he return home. His own health demanded that, too. I didn't want Doris to be the loser in another triangle, this one tragic. All my pleadings fell on deaf ears.

Suddenly I heard my name being called from the kitchen. I opened the wooden folding doors and saw Doris sitting on a bench in her red-and-white polka dot robe with a drink in her hand. "Get those people out of my house!" she demanded. She wanted his luggage brought, and it appeared she was going to have Tex stay with her, making her own claim.

"Please, Clara, let Tex get on that plane with Moury tonight," I begged. "His wife is waiting. Let Moury go with him, and get yourself out of this mess."

She refused to listen. As I left, I said, "All right, Clara, it's all in your lap now, and I'm washing my hands of this," and left with Moury and Sandy to get Tex's luggage. Things could only go from bad to worse in this predicament. Thoughts of her rendezvous with Mr. X still vivid in my mind, I worried about seeing her hurt. Why was Doris so stubborn in all of this? She wasn't even in love with Tex. What was her motivation in challenging his wife this way? I do not know to this day.

We drove to the hotel, gathered the luggage, and brought it back, taking about thirty minutes. When we arrived in the driveway, we saw a black car by the front door, and a man and Doris helping Tex into it. Once Tex was in, Doris jumped into Rack's to follow. We decided to follow, too. Nervously Moury voiced the opinion he would be hearing from Mrs. Tex. The three cars made their way down Burton Way and onto San Vincente and to the final destination—Midway Hospital.

Moury tried to call the hospital for an update before he phoned Mrs. Tex, but could not get any information. It may have been too soon, or perhaps Tex registered under an assumed name. Moury finally phoned Mrs. Tex to tell her not to go to the airport, since her husband was in the hospital.

When I got home, I decided to call Doris, concerned that she might be caught in a scandal, fighting for another woman's husband. Ruth answered and said Doris was upset, too. "I just wish Doris had put Tex on the plane and let him go home to Texas," I said. The next morning when I arrived at Doris's home, things were extremely quiet. Nobody appeared for hours, an unusual situation. I talked to Doris on the intercom a couple of times, and she seemed pleasant, but not her usual self. She expected contractors to give her an estimate on patio work, and she asked me to meet with them and get the information. Later, Ruth said she was taking Doris to the hospital to visit Tex. Doris came bouncing out, dressed in tan slacks and a comfortable top on her way to the hospital and then to Rack's for an Actors and Others Board of Directors meeting. She would be in touch.

When Ruth returned, she reported little about Doris's visit and seemed nervous and distant. I finished my chores, eager to get home to freshen up for a party with Connie Edney. I didn't want to be late. I put messages on Doris's desk and said good-bye to Alma and Ruth.

The party started at 7:30 PM and Connie greeted me, wanting me to meet some of the people she had worked with on an educational film. Many of them also worked at NBC and recognized me from the two times I had accompanied Doris when she taped the Johnny Carson show. They all made comments on her appearance on the last show, the one she had done on Labor Day in a clinging, see-through, light-blue jersey without a bra. No one missed that show!

I left the party at 9:30 PM for my apartment, fell right asleep, but was startled by the phone. The only person who called me late at night was Doris's agent, the successful president and CEO of the agency she used, who was at least 30 years older than I. I liked him, but not this side of his personality. He would keep me on the phone for at least an hour trying to proposition me. He suggested I could call him by his first name, but around Doris, I should use his complete name. I was baffled that he would spend his time bothering me, secretary to a major client. His talk on at least one occasion was quite raunchy. What kind of a person did he think I was? I was bored and offended by his obnoxious conversations. I didn't want to tell off Doris's agent. I should have hung up, but I put up with him, relieved when the conversations terminated.

The phone kept ringing, and in the darkness it took me a while to find it, expecting the lecherous agent. I glanced at my clock radio, and it read 11:30 PM. I picked up the phone; it was Ruth who sounded like a robot, "Mary Anne, I'm calling for Doris, and she doesn't want you to come to work tomorrow, and, for that matter, don't ever come back again. Please return your keys and the gate clicker to her house." I was too overcome to respond.

The painful and bitter truth I had to face was that this was not all Ruth's doing. She wouldn't have made that call without Doris's knowledge. How could the lady whom I loved and admired all these years suddenly and coldly fire me? Where was the person who wrote loving notes:

> Marzy Doats Thanks for being so damned good!!! Love you, "Clara" I adored my surprise party - I love the road runner in the tree and I'm crazy about my broom and dust pan. You're the best person I know!!! Love & Kisses, "Clara"

I took back the keys and the clicker along with a letter to Doris and gave them to Lilly at the gate. We spoke briefly, and Lilly called me later that night. She said that she gave Doris my letter and she read it immediately and broke down in tears.

I called Terry's office at RCA the next day, and Judy, his secretary, answered. As soon as she recognized my voice, she asked, "Mary Anne, where are you? Every time I call Doris's home, she always says, 'Mary Anne isn't here right now.' What's going on?" I told her. She informed me that Terry had gone out of the country for a week and that he would call when he returned. He did; I told him Doris and I had parted company. I told him I had tried to protect his mother like any friend would do, given the situation. Sadly he had no answer.

A few months later, I went to Farmer's Market and stopped by the magazine counter to look through fan/movie magazines. I picked up Rona Barrett's *Hollywood* magazine and on page six was shocked to see the following article:

THE WHOLE TOWN'S WICKED WHISPERING...about a blonde movie-TV doll (not Connie Stevens) who fired her secretary for having interfered with her private life. Story goes that Miss Movie Star has been having a hot n heavy affair with a wealthy oilinaire from Texas—very much married. And that Mr. Oilinaire came to town, got very ill at a party, which he attended with Miss Movie Star, and was rushed to the local hospital. Mr. Oilionaire's wife, of course, was notified at her Texas ranch and immediately flew to LA to be with her husband. The nurses tell me that a horrible verbal battle between the two women ensued right outside Mr. Oilinaire's sick room with Miss Movie Star leaving the hospital in disarray. Upon returning home, Miss Star fired Miss Secretary since it was Miss Secretary who had begged her boss that she not go to the hospital. As you can see loyalty in Hollywood doesn't ALWAYS pay-off!!!

I had apparently intruded in her life and embarrassed her by going too far in my advice. A month later on Thanksgiving day, Doris called. I was, of course, glad to hear her voice. "Hi, Clara, how are you? And Happy Thanksgiving!" was all I could muster. I could tell she was nervous, and so was I. We talked as if nothing had happened. I felt compelled to tell her I was her friend and always would be. With that, she broke down and said, "Mare, I know that." I added, "I just wanted you to hear that from me."

She went on, telling me about the special for CBS she was filming with John Denver. She was worn out from rehearsals, and her voice bothered her. "This is the only call I wanted to make today," she added. I wondered what that meant, but took it as an indication of affection. "Marzy, I want to talk to you. When I'm finished working on my special, I want to have a nice long talk with you, so that we can really visit." And, before we hung up, she said, "Mary Anne, I just want you to know that I love you." That long talk never happened. I didn't see her again.

From a letter from Doris December 17, 1979,

If we really want to emulate the Christ and love the way Jesus loved, then we must be forgiving, loving and compassionate. I would hope that I am a true Christian, at least I am trying.

She spoke of her ongoing interest in animal welfare, calling it "the most rewarding time I've ever done in my life." She said her dogs, Muffy, Little Tiger, Charlie, and Rudy had all gone. "Don't have to go into how difficult it was. All my angels that I love so much. I really have to do some good thinking and keep them right here with their tails wagging."

And she sent her love along with wishes for me to "stay well and happy and peaceful. You know that I wish you everything good." I wish her the same always.

Epilogue

In May, 1977, I returned to Indianapolis to start a new life with my friends, who welcomed me home. My mother was having minor health problems, and I felt it best to be with her.

During the past thirty years I have had a variety of jobs—from Director of Publicity for Perennial Pictures Film Corporation to working in the education department for Lilly Endowment. When my mother was on kidney dialysis for three-and-a-half years, I stayed home to care for her. She died at age 83, and I was grateful for those times we shared together.

For the past eight-plus years, I have been working as Development Assistant for the Little Sisters of the Poor at Saint Augustine's Home in Indianapolis. Being with the Little Sisters is a joyful experience, and I love going to work every day. These nuns bring such inspiration as they carry out their mission of caring for the elderly poor. I see miracles happen every day and feel blessed to be associated with them.

I am amazed at all the Doris Day sites on the internet. She continues to have multitudes of fans, both young and old, locally and internationally. People look up to her as a favorite and even as a role model.

As of this writing, Miss Day remains alive and well and living with her family of four-legged critters in Carmel, on a sprawling estate overlooking Pebble Beach Golf Club. She is part owner of the beautiful Cypress Inn, [www.dorisday.com], a dog-friendly hotel. Recently, she was voted the most popular movie actress of all time.

In 2004 Doris received the Presidential Medal of Freedom—the nation's highest civilian honor—not for her movie-star celebrity, but for her animal welfare work. In giving the award, President George Bush said "It was a good day for our fellow creatures when Doris gave her good heart to the cause of animal welfare."

Today Doris Day's full-time career is her work with animals and her non-profit organization, The Doris Day Animal Foundation [www.DDAF. org] established in 1996, and the Doris Day Animal League, which recently merged with the Humane Society of the United States. The Foundation pioneered "Spay Day USA," which each year coordinates low-cost spay and neuter procedures for dogs and cats nationwide. In July 2007, Doris established The Doris Day and Terry Melcher Scholarship Fund at the UC Davis Veterinary Schools to be awarded in perpetuity to outstanding veterinary students working to improve the welfare of homeless animals. Since moving to the Carmel Valley nearly 30 years ago, Doris has devoted her life and used her star-power to further animal causes.

Each year Doris Day takes an active part with Magic63, the music-of-your-life station in Carmel, [www.magic63.com] for her "All Day Doris Day Birthday Tribute." Kevin Kahl, operations manager, coordinates this special event, and on April 3, 2007, as she has done in the past, Doris called into the station three times and chatted with on-air personalities to the delight of listeners. This year Magic63 provided streaming audio so people around the world could share in Doris's world-wide celebration. Fans and friends called from Australia, England, and all across the United States to wish her happy birthday.

As I look back over the events written about in this book, I realize how fortunate I was to have been invited for a while into the life and world of Doris Day. This is one good woman.